PANDA NOT DRAGON:

WHY THE RISE OF CHINA IS NOT A THREAT

SHAOYU YUAN

For information regarding special discounts for bulk purchases, please contact 1-859-420-3263

Panda not Dragon: Why the Rise of China is not a Threat / Shaoyu Yuan
First Printing, 2019.
Manufactured in the United States of America

ISBN 978-1-5342-9990-0
Glasstree Academic Publishing

"Finishing this book will make you feel like you have been living in there for a decade. The author takes you on a journey to see China differently as the book reveals much of the unheard truth to the Westerners."
--- The Global Affairs

"...a must read for anyone who is interested in Asian geo-politics or the economic challenges and opportunities presented by China's emergence on a global scale. It has the potential to revolutionise how Western governments and businesses deal with Chinese growth."
--- Best in Australia

"Spellbinding reading that starts with explaining 'traditional' Xenophobia and Sinophobia in the West and opens up on a veritable encyclopedia of China's strengths, challenges, aspirations, and dreams. It brings as much light into the opaqueness of Chinese politics as a young scholar who loves his country and people could marshal without falling foul of the guardians of political correctness. A compact introduction to China in the era of intercontinental competition!"
--- Dr. Friedrich Lohr, Former German Ambassador to North Korea, Delegate to the United Nations.

CONTENTS

ACKNOWLEDGEMENTS

As an international student to the United States from China, I was able to experience the differences between these two great countries. I was able to watch the Kentucky Derby and tell the thrill of gambling and betting on horses to folks in China. I was able to drink alcohol whenever I want even as an underage in China and flaunt about it to my American friends. But most importantly, I was able to dive into and explore the distinction of two political systems, two types of economies, and the two wonderful cultures cultivated very diversely. I feel fortunate, and so should any other international students.

Undergoing the American education, the more I learn the more I realize that what I comprehend will never be enough for anything, and throughout the writing, I often wonder who am I to determine, to predict, and even to observe the fate of two great nations. But that is fine because a part of the development of humankind's apprehension of knowledge is based on sharing what you found and put it out there for criticisms.

My research might be shallow, and my thoughts might be naïve, but I am always on the path of learning new things and becoming a more knowledgeable person. My undergraduate, Centre

College, and the esteemed professors there are almost everything that made me a better person and a scholar. My works and I might never be perceived as good enough, but it is certain that things would be much worse if Centre College was not my Alma mater.

Mr. Karlin Chang, my graduate school Northeastern University, and Boston University provided much information and access to their holdings. My little brother, Nathan Anthony Herl, thank you for your dedication. My dear friend, Shichao Jia, has assisted me with the searching and making of data and graphs throughout the book. Many thanks to George Sampson, Andrew Belson, Chimao Lin, Aigul Khairulla, Leili Niu, Nicholas Johnson, and Dr. Jiseo Kim, Dr. Fiona Creed, who assisted me in various respects during the journey of writing the manuscripts. Special thanks to Dr. Michael Dixon, Dr. Vitaly Kozyrev, Ambassador Friedrich Lohr, Professor Zhenlin Zhang, Mr. Karlin Chang, Professor Sean Xia, and Dr. Shiva Ayyadurai, who inspired me enormously in many ways. My greatest gratitude is to my lovely girlfriend, Yeonsoo Kim, who accompanied me through every page of this book.

I dedicate this book to my family.

PREFACE

Why China? These two words have been the rhetorical question to many statements regarding the issues related to China. To many, especially Americans, their impressions of the country are still rather unclear. 'I am going to move to China,' 'Why China?' 'The 2022 Winter Olympics is going to be held in China,' 'Why China?' The reason that people are having doubts about China is not because of their lack of knowledge of the nation, but rather their knowledge of China is mostly based on films, news, and other forms of media, which are something that other people wanted you to see, not what you have seen in your eyes, and that is dangerous. The same applies to the question of 'Is the rise of China a threat to the world? '; the answer is no. To those who say 'Yes,' me as a person who was born and raised in China, can assure you that the rise of China is rather peaceful, and the conclusion of a 'Yes' is practically extrapolated on misconceptions.

Indeed, China is rising, and it is rising in an unprecedented manner, however, by 'unprecedented', it is only to Western society; the expeditious rise of a nation which is located in neither Europe nor America, believes in neither democracy nor capitalism, serves as a disturbance to the West, principally to the United States. Nevertheless, this apprehension of China's rising is unfounded. Fear to the danger is often greater than the danger itself, not to mention that, in this case, danger does not exist. Nowadays, in a time of admiring science and seeking the truth, if we are to validate a hypothesis, observations must be made objectively. In this instance, the statement, 'the rise of China is a threat to the world' is the hypothesis that will ultimately be proven incorrect, and many Western scholars are looking at the supposition subjectively, only from the eyes of the West.

China is rising in a unipolar world where the US, a Western, democratic country serves as the one and only world 'police,' and this situation of having only one superpower in the entire planet has never happened before in human history. The West underwent two World Wars and the Cold War, fought off Imperialism, Fascism, and Communism; ever since the end of the Cold War, the US, and the West are situated in a state of 'enemy-lessness.' It is this state of 'enemy-lessness' that causes many Westerners to be unable to examine the rise of China objectively, overlooking many of the most important facts of China. In order to interpret my contention, we shall look at the rise of China from within, economically and militarily, soft power and hard power, not just from the Western point of view.

'What comes next then? If a rising China is not to be worried', one may ask. We are living in the greatest time of history; human civilization has never been this developed, and the world has never been this connected before. We now understand that cursing is bad, killing is wrong, and there are endangered animals we need to protect. All of these values we believe in today did not happen because of how evil we are; they happened because human beings are well beyond killing for needs. China's growing economy is helping the world to eliminate poverty and famines, and the technology that China has 'copied' and improved are eventually sharing back to where they originated because of the advancement of technology and how connected we are. If the concern is that China's economy will eventually surpass that of the United States, this book will assure you that the day is still far from us, while China is not fit for conflict, that day might just not come. With what I mentioned above, I see the rise of China as a peaceful opportunity which every country can and should take 'advantage' of, and it is not a threat to be concerned.

CHAPTER I

THE HISTORY OF SINOPHOBIA

To understand how the West views China and why the West views China in a certain way, we must understand the history behind it. Xenophobia is not a modern invention, which can trace back to thousands of years ago, when the ancient Greeks first called the foreigners as 'barbarians'; the judgement that those who share inferior culture than the Greeks are destined to be enslaved, which I consider as the first time that the Europeans 'belittled' others. It is common that people do not like one another, but whenever a person or a group with a different background shows up, the spearhead often turns to the outsider. From a micro-perspective, in a basketball match between class A and class B, the students would fight for their classes and the title of a 'better class,' and the students would look down to those who are from the different class. In a national level basketball game, the students in these two classes would play together as one team for their school and see the other schools as their enemies. When the games escalate to the world level, all the schools in the nation will unite together to select the best players to play for the nation. In the match between the two classes, to class A, class B is 'foreign' and animus. In the national level match, class A and class B belong to the same school, and together they view the other schools as 'foreign.' People will always find ways to define who the outsider is and find common traits to decide who should be on the same side. When it goes beyond basketball games, to culture and security, humankind takes sides in a bigger perspective; identity becomes the ultimate factor that decides who you are with. Identity consists of countless elements that depend on the defining situation, but in this case, nationality, skin color, religion, language, and even appearance grow into the components for us to justify which group we belong to. When the Europeans and Asians discovered each other, just as the time when German and French were scorning each other over their differences, the conflicts with the neighbors seem rather frivolous; a group of others that looks different, speaks disparate languages, practices contrasting beliefs, is more likely to be the pernicious antagonist. The hatred and fear of the oriental people became more and more racial, rather than national.

If you watch the alien pranks videos uploaded on the internet, you will notice that the first reaction when people see an alien is to run for their lives, none dared to communicate with the 'aliens,' which implies that people automatically presumed these human-shaped creatures as a danger to their lives. A very similar situation occurred after the increment of communication between white people and East Asians, which brings us a new form of Xenophobia, categorically to the people of East Asia.

THE YELLOW PERIL

The term 'Yellow Peril' itself is a product of a time when race perfectly blended into the concept of nationalism. The phrase was first manufactured by the French Russian sociologist Yakov Novikov. Later years in the 19th century, the German Kaiser Wilhelm II famously used the term to inspire his fellow European nations to attack and encroach the Far East, specifically China. At the time of a burgeoning Europe and its hunger for resources, when the king of one of the most powerful empires in the world encourages his men to invade a land of aliens, there was no reason to not to differentiate and discriminate the East Asians. Colonization became the justification for the Europeans to deal with the Yellow Peril. Creating and implementing the concept of 'Yellow Terror,' the Europeans made China a place which all white men should step up and ravage before the yellow men became a threat to their women and land. The pillaging and destruction of the 'Garden of all Gardens', Old Summer Palace, by the British and French, already demonstrated the attitude of the European soldiers to the Orientals. After the concept of Yellow Peril was ingrained in the minds of the West, the Siege of the International Legations happened at the beginning of the 20th century

17

seemed less of a surprise. Eight countries invaded China, in the name of eradicating the Boxers; ended with the occupation of the capital city Peking, the Westerners turned the invasion of Peking to an outrageous 'orgy of looting and violence' by not only soldiers but also the missionaries and journalists. At that time, plundering in China was the fashion trend for foreigners. On a side note, Imperial Japan was among the eight countries that ravaged Peking. The stronger-than-ever, newly industrialized nation did not care about its fellow East Asian country, instead, after the defeat over Qing Dynasty in the first Sino-Japanese War, Japan thought to estrange itself from the Yellow Peril, claiming to be not only Western but also a white country.

Once the mighty Qing Dynasty was defeated multiple times by the Europeans, and specifically by the Japanese, the empire seemingly lost all of its respect; several unequal treaties were signed with Western countries with no defiance from the Qing government. On the other side of the ocean, the United States, Australia, and Canada became the destinations for many Chinese immigrants in the 19th century. Perhaps, because of the servility cultivated by thousands of years of dynastic feudalism, the Chinese immigrants willingly accepted much lower compensations with excessive working hours, automatically made themselves the second-class citizens. These two factors, together with the already existing racism, outlawed the previous signed Burlingame Treaty (between the U.S. and China) which was the first equal agreement signed with a Western country since the Second Opium War, and

18

replaced it with what I call the first official acts of Sinophobia, the Page Act of 1875 and the Chinese Exclusion Act of 1882, as the first US law to restrain people of a certain ethnic or nation from immigrating. These two acts were signed to last ten years; however, kudos to how deep-seated Sinophobia was in the United States, the act was first renewed and then became permanent law in the year of 1902.

Around the same time, the federal government of Australia embraced the White Australia Policy which was designd to prevent the people of non-European origins, primarily pointing to the East Asians, from migrating to Australia; the adoption of this policy later prompted the birth of Immigration Restriction Act 1901. To the north of America, the Canadians also passed a law, the Chinese Exclusion Act, restricting almost all the forms of immigration from China. The end of the 19th century and the beginning of the 20th century was the peak of Sinophobia. It seemed like bashing on China and its people were contributing to world peace. The point here is not how many Western countries implemented the laws on restricting Chinese immigrants; what is crucial is that we must remember that Yellow Peril racism was more than substantial, fear and antipathy to the yellow men did not happen after China started to rise. It was there hundreds of years ago, and Western nations actually took domestic actions and poured gas onto the fire of Yellow Terror. Since this kind of law prevailed for decades in a time that's not too far from where we are now, the influence and remnants of these legislations are still in existence. When something is prohibited in the law, you know it is terrible for you. I understand why many believe the rise of China is threatening, but one must understand that the vestiges of the Yellow Peril are still here, and they have been contributing to the mistaken belief, not factual evidence.

INFLUENCE OF MASS MEDIA

The United States, the homeland of the world's largest film industry in terms of revenue, is also one of the few countries that started to produce movies at the beginning of the 20th century. Film is a European invention, and it is understandable to only see white people in the cinema, given the circumstances at that time. However, we are living in a modern society, and the first time we see an all Asian-cast Hollywood film on screen was in 1995. Ironically, the second time we see an all Asian-cast movie is 25 years later, in 2018, the very same year as the year I am writing this book. Only two all Asian-cast films were made in Hollywood in over a hundred years of film making history. This does not mean that Asian people do not watch movies; it implies that either seeing Asian faces on screen make people uncomfortable, or Hollywood simply does not like Asians. Perhaps it is both, but how did this even happen in the 21st century? The mass media itself, particularly Western media, is one of the many answers that caused people having a hard time watching an Asian man kissing a white woman on screen.

Let us look at the actual influence of the media. A couple of pages of paper may seem very simple and trivial, but the information on the paper is authoritative, especially when the same set of paper are printed to circulate amongst the mass. The news and information you see do not come out of your body like the food; instead, they stay in your brain. People may not realize their brains remembered what they read because most of the information is only stored subconsciously, but they are there. False and illusive information are very much like brain parasites, they will not kill you, however, the next time your brain receives something related to the false information you read before, the false information comes out as preconceptions to affect the way you think, and eventually, these messages will change your belief. Another alarming matter that most people do not realize is the danger of the combination of preconception created by false information and the gregarious nature of human beings. Friends associate, family gathers, and most importantly, children stay with their parents. When a piece of misleading information preconceive a parent's mind, the message passes on to the children through daily family time, and the kids will discharge what they learned in home to their friends; information is too 'contagious' among us that sometimes we do not even comprehend how catching it is.

Starting from the earliest form of media, newspaper, in this case, is also fair enough to call it propaganda when it is used to depict anything foreign-related, with both images and words. John Mearsheimer, in his *The Tragedy of Great Power Politics*, indicates that states can never be certain about each other's motives.

Indeed, we cannot be sure about other's intentions because we are not others, and media companies, often controlled by the government at that time, are no exceptions. The newspaper officer would often print what the government tells them to print; therefore, the audience would only see what the controller of media wants them to see. If a nation wants to start a war, the media insinuates the justification for the war through paper, making people either support the war or providing them with necessities of starting the war. The Yellow Peril racism was the model product of European's invasion plan to Asia.

Völker Europas, Wahrt Eure Heiligsten Güter (Folks of European Nations, Protect Your Beloved Goods), by Hermann Knackfuß.

The figure shown is a drawing by German painter Hermann Knackfuß, one of the most classic propaganda, providing the justification for invading China. On the left side of the painting, European nations are interpreted as white women with arms, protected by Saint Michael the Archangel who is pointing his hand to the east with his other hand holding the sword. On the right side of the painting, across the land and river, the sky is saturated with smoke, and a flaming Buddha is siding with the Chinese dragon, gawking the Archangel and the women he is defending. Needless to explain the representations and the insinuation, Kaiser Wilhelm II himself commissioned the painting to advocate the concept of Yellow Peril, paving the road for the European invasion of China. Below is another example of drawings that promotes the Yellow Peril racism in.

Mongolian Octopus: Its Grip on Australia, by Phil May

Paintings and drawings that are similar to this started to appear consistently in Europe and the US, and the image of the Orient was officially constructed; not discriminating against Asians seemed illogical in that time. Along with the racist policies promulgated by the Western countries, these images and words branded into people's head. With the power of media and the gregarious nature of humankind, these impressions of China and its people did not die in a century; on the contrary, they became one of the main reasons that people would perceive the rise of China as a threat to the West.

The Yellow Peril racism advanced with the development of technology, in forms of media. Like I mentioned above, the first all Asian-cast film was not on the screen until 1995 and the second one did not come out until this year (2018), while Asian American represents nearly 6 percent of the US population. Of course, not having all-Asian cast films does not represent racism; however, many of the films that have Asian characters in them are more discriminating than we think. Take Dr. Fu Manchu for an example, created by English novelist Sax Rohmer. Fu Manchu is a Chinese criminal who wants to take over the world with his crazy science. Fu Manchu was featured in multiple novels and movies, representing the face of Yellow Terror. The existence of Fu Manchu was to remind the white audiences that there is always a yellow devil in the east that could hurt your family and possessions. Fu Manchu still appears in movies occasionally, and people seem to mostly accept it, however, a seemingly insignificant implication, 'Chinese is evil' is also plugged into the viewer's head. A contradictory character to Fu Manchu, Charlie Chan created by Hollywood, a supposedly heroic Chinese American detective. The character and its movies seemed like an effort to offset the Yellow Peril racism displayed in Fu Manchu films; nevertheless, the real discrimination and racism is that neither Fu Manchu nor Charlie Chan was played by actual Asian actors in most of the adapted films. Almost all of them were portrayed by white actors, with the slanted eyes makeups and yellow cosmetics, which successfully prevented the implication of 'Chinese is not evil' from plugging into people's head.

The phenomena are also common among recent films. The film-making companies often replace Asian characters as written in the novel and comic books with Caucasian actors, 'whitewashing' the movie. For instance, Marvel's blockbuster Doctor Strange casted actress Tilda Swinton to portray the Ancient One, an Asian male from the Tibetan area. Most recently, Death Note, a Netflix film adapted from one of the most popular manga in Japan, completely replaced the leading role with Caucasian actors. Today, it is still very difficult for an average American to name even one Hollywood male Asian actors' name other than Jackie Chan who is primarily known for his Kungfu moves. Are audiences really that uncomfortable with seeing leading roles played by Asians in films? We do not know, but we do know is that 'whitewashing' a film diminishes the chances of seeing a positive Asian image on screen, which could potentially lead to bias against the group.

THE PSYCHOLOGY BEHIND

Things happen for a reason, and people act based on motives. The apparent reason for Europeans to forge the Yellow Peril ideology was to justify the invasion and colonization of East Asia; however, we barely see any 'justifications' and propaganda of colonizing Africa and South America, and let us be honest, the effort made on defaming the people of East Asia is too much. There was something more than just the need for resources and expansion; that is the combination of cultural fear, sexual fear, and xenophobia, which can be explained from a psychological perspective.

The European colonists started to colonize Africa and Latin America before they planned anything in East Asia, certainly not as they did not discover Asia first, but because they were uncertain of the strength and power of the region at that time. Marco Polo, although not the first European to arrive in Asia, was the first traveler who documented his over two decades of journey in China and other Asian countries. Regardless of the dispute of whether he served as the Governor of Hangzhou and an advisor to Kublai Khan or not, Marco Polo comprehensively chronicled the wealth and civilization he witnessed in the East, expressing his awe and amazement of the grandeur of China. His book became famous, and his story got told; European nations could only wish to achieve the same prosperity of China. The reason I brought up the travels of Marco Polo is to remind us that the Europeans did not view the East Asians as the ugly barbarian and savages in the beginning, on the contrary, many documents in China recorded the white people from the West as uncultured barbarians. So, what made the Europeans changed their views?

Henry the Navigator, the Portuguese Prince who 'discovered' West Africa, and Christopher Columbus, the Spanish Pioneer, unlike Marco Polo, did not come back to Europe with the information and notes that describe the wealth and greatness of the places they explored; instead, Henry and Columbus brought back Europe the 'key' to the era of colonization and exploration, because they did not see any formidable strength and power in Latin American and Sub-Saharan Africa that could stop them from invading and enslaving the indigenous people. Once the land was easily invaded and colonized, the local culture and religion were automatically recognized as weaker, inferior, and less advanced compared to those of Europe. Therefore, the Caucasian nations had no worries that one day, these 'barbarians' would become more developed and invade Europe. However, on the other side, the far East was presented as this mysterious yet formidable and affluent region, which was certainly not an excellent choice to invade, not until centuries later.

A couple of hundreds of years later, the Europeans experienced the Industrial Revolution while the Chinese were still living in the joy of feudalism. Three centuries of development have completely turned the table for the world; Europeans were driving steamboats and producing goods with machines, whereas the Chinese emperors were immersed in his illusions of the might of the 'Central

Empire' composed with wooden ships, spear-using soldiers, and agricultural products. At that time, the Europeans still see and respect China as a powerful empire, and China still views the Europeans as uncultured and underdeveloped barbarians. However, things started to change since the Macartney Mission. In the late 18th century, China and the East seemed like the only few places the British have not yet exploited on this planet. Lord Macartney was sent to China to start the first British diplomatic mission, aiming to achieve a few goals including the new openings of trading ports and a permanent establishment of the British embassy in the capital of China. Although all of the objectives were failed to achieve, this mission provided a closer look of China to the Europeans, making them realize that China might not be the same as it used to be documented in the travels of Marco Polo.

Our Celestial Empire possesses all things in prolific abundance and lacks no product within its borders. There is therefore no need to import the manufactures of outside barbarians in exchange for our own produce.
— Qianlong Emperor, Letter to King George III of Great Britain, 1792.

Together with the arrogance and extreme confinement of the Canton system to foreign traders, the European imperialism and expansionism eventually led to the Opium Wars with China. The Opium Wars did not fully make the Westerners realize how weak the Qing Empire was; the First Sino-Japanese War proclaimed to the world how feeble China has become. After that, the Western world went on utterly aggressive on China; China was forced to sign various unequal treaties and cede parts of its territory, which finally brings to my point. The Europeans believed that China could, once again, became dominant and outpaced the West with its completely different religion, culture, and blood. They have seen what the yellow people were able to achieve, and the western powers saw this as an opportunity to prevent China from spreading its culture, getting back on its feet, and eventually assimilating or eradicating the Western culture. The size and population of China were also among the factors that caused the cultural fear, concerning that the yellow race had stronger reproductive advantages, which also served as the sexual fear that mixed-race children, the combination of white and yellow, whose existence would threaten the properness of whiteness. Another aspect of the sexual fear is that the affluent and erudite Asian male could easily corrupt the white females, and with the sexual voracity of Asian people, the white race and culture of Christian West could eventually be assimilated by the yellow race and the oriental civilization, which certainly seems impossible nowadays; while Asian males are recognized as the least attractive group for dating today, the Yellow Peril ideology has been very successful so far from the perspective of sexual fear.

THE WAY OF CHINA

Chinese, especially Han Chinese, is a rather peaceful group of people, and the history of China along with its current policy substantiate this inference.

29

Throughout the thousands of years of Chinese history, the country certainly had many dynasties. However, its territory did not expand much at all when the Han Chinese were in control, and war happened much less frequent compared with European nations; the country was more defensive than aggressive. People often joke about the Great Wall of China, calling it the only Chinese product that lasted for so long, which made it one of the world's seven wonders, but jokes aside, we must understand the Great Wall itself serves as a symbol of the non-aggressiveness of China. The wall was initially constructed to stop the Xiongnu people from invading the Qin Dynasty, and Qin Shi Huang, the first Chinese emperor, was not the only Chinese emperor who adopted the wall strategy to keep them secured. The Great Wall was continuously being rebuilt, enhanced during many dynasties, until the Ming Dynasty which was the last dynasty that was controlled by the Han Chinese. The Great Wall and its relations with these dynasties of China are straightforward; whenever the Han Chinese were in control, they maintained and reinforced the wall to protect themselves, but whenever the non-Han ethnics took over China, they always expanded beyond China and East Asia. When Kublai Khan conquered the Southern Song Dynasty, the Mongol empire became the largest contiguous land empire in human history, ranging from today's Korea to the east of Europe. Qing Dynasty, established by the Manchurians, developed into one of the largest empires in the world in the 18th century, after the conquests in central Asia, au contraire, the dynasties which established by the Han Chinese were invariably focused on the development of economy, art, and science, for example, all the Four Great Inventions were invented during dynasties built by Han Chinese, and among these inventions, two of them originated from the Song Dynasty which was one of the most unwarlike dynasties in China.

Another example of the nonassertive nature of Han Chinese is the multiple treasure voyages happened during Ming Dynasty which was the last dynasty that established and controlled by the Han Chinese. The voyages were a total of seven sea expeditions led by Admiral Zheng He and his fleet of Ming treasure ships. Let us look at the sizes of the fleets in the voyages. The first voyage included at least 60 treasure ships and at least 25,000 crew members, and the second voyage consisted of over two hundred treasure ships, although the historians are still debating about the number of ships over the next a few voyages, the size and the amount of the treasure ships were unprecedentedly large, and the seventh voyage contained at least over a hundred large vessels. Undoubtedly, the voyages and fleet made Ming the most potent naval power in the 15th century. With these many fleets and such a maritime power, one would think that the proprietor of such a dominion was planning invasion and expansion. However, the most that Emperor Yongle and the Chinese wanted was a suzerainty in the known world; the nature of these voyages was rather diplomatic and commercial. The Ming Dynasty, preceded by Yuan Dynasty of the Mongols, and succeeded by the Qing Dynasty of Manchurians, had one of the most limited territories compare to the other dynasties of China. Instead of going to total war with the Mongols and Manchus, the Ming dynasty, ruled by the Han people, adopted the Great Wall strategy, constructing stronger and much more elaborate walls of bricks and stones. Although continuing the construction of the Great Wall and not invading other nations with its powerful navy cannot determine the nature of an ethnicity, it does reflect a particular pattern of the group's stance, and in this case, China was never an expansionist.

As for today, the Chinese government did not even give any official response to the ideology of Yellow Peril, nor did the Chinese come up with any racism against the white nations. I am not suggesting that there are no human rights problems that exist in China; I am only referring to the nation's foreign policy and its almost blank dissemination of depreciating other cultures. In fact, the Chinese name of United States means the 'beautiful country,' the United Kingdom translates to a 'heroic country'; people of China hold very high respect to Western cultures and ideologies. Unlike the United States, the new China prefers to mind its own business and advocates that countries should not be meddling with each other's domestic affairs like civil wars, human rights issues, and social instabilities. Indeed, when it comes to decision-making time in the United Nations, China often abstains its vote, and the last war China ever had ended around 40 years ago, the Sino-Vietnamese War, which concluded with the Chinese withdrawal from Vietnam, failing to avert the Vietnamese from Cambodia. Among the Five Nuclear Weapon States (United States, United Kingdom, Russia, France, and China) under the

Treaty on the Non-Proliferation of Nuclear Weapons (NPT), China is the only nation that declared its policy of No First Use of nuclear weapons; at least, the world does not have to worry about a nuclear attack launched by China. Apropos of the foreign policy and military situations, we shall discuss more in the following chapters.

To end this chapter, I wish to share a few questions that I often get asked by my American and European friends when I just arrived in Kentucky, as a Chinese student. "Do you eat dogs? If so, you need to tell your countrymen to stop eating our cute friends." I certainly don't eat dogs, same as most of the Chinese people. "Does it bother you that Cowan (the school cafeteria) don't often serve any rice dishes?" Well, it does sometimes because I personally like rice, but people from many other parts of China do not see rice as a main dish. "How come your eyes aren't slanted?" We all have slanted eyes, and it just depends on the angle. "You have to teach me Kungfu, so I can survive and talk to the Chinese if China invades us." I do not know Kungfu, and China will not invade the United States; neither does it have the need nor the ability. I was told that many of these questions are based on racism and stereotypes, and it is wrong for anyone to think like this. Their thoughts are undoubtedly incorrect, but I don't blame them, and they are not born racist for asking these questions, instead, the reason that there are still so many people who do not understand China or misjudge China is that the ideology of the Yellow Peril created a century ago is still in existence through media, and the rise of China is providing an opportunity for this racial bigotry to revive, justifying the threat of China, thus forged a new wave of Sinophobia among the rest of the world, especially in the Western nations.

CHAPTER II

THE CHINESE ECONOMY AND SOCIAL STABILTY: IS CHINA PREPARED FOR A CONFLICT?

We all know that China is now the second largest economy in this world, but we should not be surprised considering the size and population of the country, and gross domestic product should not be the only index to value a country's economic power; there are many other factors to consider, along with social elements. To claim a country as a threat, it must have the capacity to compete with its adversaries, with a truly stable society and structure; if to rival with the United States, China cannot yet play the attrition warfare due to its status quo of social and economic issues. Greater social inequality leads to greater social instability, which makes the country an unstable economy, not suitable for a conflict.

Before Former President Deng Xiaoping's economic reform and opening-up policy, China was engaged in a planned economy. The whole society and social structure were rather identical. Ever since Deng's economic reform, with the progress of globalization, the Chinese economy started to become more diversified. To embrace the opportunities brought by globalization, the Deng administration decided to let the small and medium enterprises "fly," loosening the requirements to start businesses and providing incentives for them to attract foreign investment rather than controlling and directing them. The Chinese government aided the state-owned enterprises to form monopolies in their industries. In the 1990s, these state-owned companies such as PetroChina, China Telecom, started to grow with remarkable speed, dominating their fields in China, and eventually became one of the main features of the "socialism with Chinese characteristics." What is different from the other major economies in the world is that the public sectors in China are responsible for a much larger share of the economy compared to the growing private sectors. With the continuing development of society, China again welcomed the opportunities brought by globalization in the 2000s. The country embraced an average GDP growth of 10% for more than 30 years, remained as the fastest growing economy on this planet until 2015. However, along with the supposedly "socialism with Chinese characteristics," opportunities and benefits are not the only things brought to China; there are unfortunate social phenomena and unprecedented problems behind the glamorous development numbers.

THE LOPSIDED EDUCATIONAL OPPORTUNITIES

Since Deng instituted the market reform, households in China have been significantly aided, along with the tremendous drop in poverty numbers. Nevertheless, in excess of the reduced poverty and urbanization, in the very meantime, the income gap has escalated vastly, which accounts for one of the most significant factors of social inequality in China. Rising from 34.9% in 1995 to 53.3% in 2010, the Gini Coefficient of China gives us a general idea of how much the income gap has increased. The disparities of earnings are very special and somewhat complicated in China, due to the geography and demography of the nation; the distinctions of living standards indicate the income inequality plainly between rural and urban areas, coastal and landlocked regions, in addition to the inequality between Han Chinese and other ethnic minorities. Deng's famous quote "In order to make everyone rich, we must let some people get rich first" not only corresponded with his policies but also dovetailed with an aphorism by the English poet Percy Shelley, "The rich get richer, and the poor get poorer." Indeed, the income gap went up drastically since the market reform, the rich were able to obtain more resources, receiving better education and healthcare, while the impoverished mostly stayed at the bottom of the country's social ladder; higher education background usually lands one a higher pay, and the higher salary prepares the tuition of an even better education for the next generation, on the other hand, the poor could barely afford monthly bills with the basic livelihood, not to mention paying for education, thus causing a vicious circle. Not many people could escape the vicious circle, and the Chinese even created terms for those men and women of low-income families who successfully went to higher education and became well-paid, calling them 'Phoenix Man' or 'Phoenix Woman,' referring them as the phoenixes flew out of the petty birds.

I remember when my father used to tell me this story of one of his younger friends whom he met at his first job in a steel mill in Inner Mongolia to remind me to cherish his open-mindedness and unbraced support to my decisions. His name is Feng, born in a small village that is dozens of miles away from our hometown Ulanhad, called Harqin Banner. Feng was smart and ambitious, but his family was poor and very close-minded. After six years of compulsory (tuition-free) education he received in Ulanhad where he had to walk over six hours to school, Feng was told to stay at home and help out with family matters. Feng wanted to go to college and become an architect. However, he had no choice but to come back to the village due to financial problems. Feng's family believed that spending money on schools was nothing compared to farming and selling vegetables. Because of his family and his belief in filial piety, Feng decided to stay at home and not to go to junior high school; he wanted to save money first and go to schools when he had enough. Unlike what we often see in the movies, Feng never got enough money to go to school, and he eventually stayed at Harqin for almost ten years, until his father died of diseases. Thereafter, Feng left the village and came to the city of Ulanhad where he met my father and shared the story, and he was too old to go to school after that. I do not know how accurate the story is, after all, my father was only telling me this story to appreciate his broad-mindedness and support, but I do understand the meaning behind the story; I probably would not have been in America if my father did not go to higher education and really learned about the United States. My point is that the market reform did not reform people's way of thinking; a narrow mind remains narrow, and a broad mind does not become 'cramped.' When the narrow minds account for a more significant share in the family, the next generation is likely to share the same outlook, while the different voice is likely to get held down by the family and gradually become one of them. A society cannot fully progress if such phenomenon continues to exist.

Feng's story happened decades ago, but I soon came to realize that families like Feng's still exist, and there are still a lot of them in China. In fact, Feng was considered fortunate to enjoy public funding for his early education in the urban area. In mainland China, rural education was highly neglected due to the government's concentration on prompt economic growth, and urban education often gets more awareness and financing from the central government. For those rural families that live even further from the urban region, the already severe situation in addition to the deficient in government funding portent that these children had to give up schools. In 2017, based on the United Nations Population Division's World Urbanization Prospects, the World Bank estimates that there is still over 40 percent of the population in China dwelling in rural areas. Because of the unequal educational opportunities, many of these children end up doing the same thing as their parents do for livings, with barely any opportunities of forwarding movement in their life.

With the rough environment in the rural area and the absence of educational conditions, teachers tend to leave the rural region and choose to teach in urban divisions where schools offer higher wages and better benefits, along with the abundant educational resources. Such contradistinction between rural and urban sectors induced to a phenomenon that schools in rural areas cannot find enough qualified teachers, which widens the already large gap in instructor preparation between the two sectors. Many rural students already dropped out of schools due to the conditions mentioned above, and for those who were able to finish schools in the rural regions, they do not consider themselves as competitive applicants for top university admissions. In addition to rural student's qualifications for college admissions and jobs, the Hukou system of China also stands in the way of advancement. The Hukou system identifies each person or family as a resident of a specific area in order to restrict massive migration, which not only categorizes the quality of education and healthcare given to the urban and rural citizens but also provides difficulties for rural citizens that wish to migrate to a city with better education or find an urban occupation. Although the Chinese government has been tackling these inequalities created by the Hukou system through new policies, the situation does not seem like it is going to change much for the migrants. As a result, there have been less and less students from rural regions who get admitted to the country's leading universities like Tsinghua University and Peking University. For example, if a student with their hukou registered in Beijing, it is much easier for them to get admitted to universities in Beijing than those who have their hukou registered outside of Beijing and rural areas, consequently, rural students must work a lot harder and score much higher than students with a hukou of Beijing on the National College Entrance Examination (the Gaokao test) to get into universities in Beijing where there is a cluster of top universities in the country.

Education is the most fundamental element of development, and China still has a long way to go, while the United States is known for its most advanced education system in the world. If a country has not yet even solved the most fundamental problem of equal education, how can this country be viewed as a threat to other security?

THE PUBLIC RESTROOM THEORY

Lilian Lee is one of the most prominent female TV writers in China, but there is a paragraph in one of her prose books called Lü Yao (綠腰) or Green Waist when translated in English; the paragraph itself has become more famous than herself to Chinese academics. Her exact words are, and I translate, "To understand the level of education of one country, we must look at its public restrooms; to see the taste of a man, we must look at his socks...to see the relationship of two individuals, we must look at the level of nervousness of him or her when an accident happened to the other person." The first time I read this paragraph, I was confused but intrigued by it. The public restroom thing did not make sense to me at first, however, after recalling all the public restrooms experience which I have had around the world, it started to seem like a plausible theory to me.

I was born in China, living in the United States now, other than a few European and Southeast Asian countries I have traveled, I have also spent a decent amount of time living in Japan and South Korea for various reasons. Among all these countries, the restrooms in Japan impressed me the most. As we all have seen or heard, the nation's smart toilet warms your seat and cleans up the business automatically with no need for toilet paper. You would assume that this kind of toilets only exists in the high-end places and the home of rich people, however, the smart toilet is rather common in Japan; I was fortunate enough to enjoy the convenience of these automatic toilets everywhere I went including a village outside of Yamaguchi city. Inner Mongolia, where I was born, always give me the most unpleasant toilet experience which made almost every toilet I used in other countries a blessed experience. Most of the toilets in the villages and minor cities of China are basically large holes built on a platform above a pool of stools, with no toilet paper provided, no privacy covers, and no ways to flush, while the toilets in the Bluegrass Airport at Lexington Kentucky make me feel the most 'comfortable'. In fact, the toilet condition remains the same even for some areas in the capital of China. I often compare Kentucky with Inner Mongolia, both places are regularly described by people as 'the middle of nowhere' and are famous for their horses. Although Inner Mongolia is much larger in size, with way more population than Kentucky, the GDP of the Chinese autonomous region in 2017 only topped that of Kentucky by less than 50 billion of dollars, which certainly seems implausible if you look at the difference of the land sizes and the population between these two states. Many may claim that this comparison is rather unfair and irresponsible since China is still developing, however, if we are to describe China as a threat, there's nothing wrong with the comparison. This contrast tells us two things, first of all, total GDP does not indicate how developed an area is; secondly, the average quality of toilets can tell a lot about the level of development of a place.

The quality of the restrooms is often the least thing people care about when there are bigger problems a country needs to solve, while if a government has the luxury to upgrade its public restrooms across the state, the country should be quite developed. Of course, I did not and cannot check every single toilet in any of these countries mentioned, and the level of development can never be determined by a single factor, thus the public restroom theory will always stay as a theory, however, the top countries in the ranking of Human Development Index do tend to have nicer public restrooms, and I genuinely feel that this would be an interesting theory to share with the readers of this book as a side note.

THE INCOMING BUBBLE COLLAPSE

I am not a 'bubble theorist' who believes that China's economy has become a giant bubble which will burst soon, however, in this case, I am referring to the incoming collapse of China's housing market which is practically a bubble that has been inflating for years, and a soon-to-collapse housing market indicates an unhealthy economy. China's real estate market has been an important driver of the economic growth of the country. Nevertheless, bearish forecasts for the property market in China has been increasing unprecedentedly in recent years. Inside the bubble, the recent aggravation of the dissimilitude in China's housing market has created a total 'chaos'; housing supply has outstripped demand considerably, while the property prices in first-tier cities like Beijing and Shanghai have skyrocketed but the cost for similar properties in smaller cities have been plummeting. Meanwhile, most young people in China still could not afford a place to live.

The status quo of China's housing market is looking more and more similar to that of the US before 2008. According to the 100 City Price Index issued by China Index Academy, from 2015 to 2017, the price per square foot has skyrocketed to over 200 USD, representing a 31% increase from previous years. As for the US, the current median list price per square foot is only at 151 USD. The vast contrast does not

44

stop here. While the price per square foot remains high in China, China's Gross national income (GNI) per capita is only 16,760 USD, representing less than 30% of the GNI per capita of the US. Just as conjectured, owning a property has become an impossible dream for most Chinese people. The central government has been trying hard to remedy the situation; however, the fact that the Chinese government is taking serious actions proves that the skyrocketing property prices are not just the result of a genuine surge in demand.

What are the causes of such a phenomenon? 'Rome' was not built in a day, analogously, the giant bubble was inflated by more than one factor. The root of all 'evil' started from the government's extreme reliance on land sale for its income. If you are not familiar with the history of Communist China, you might be wondering how come the government owns all the land. During the end of the Chinese Civil War, Chairman Mao Zedong launched a campaign of land reform (土地改革). The goal was to redistribute the land owned by the rich to the peasants. However, the way used to achieve this goal turned out to be a campaign of mass murder of landlords. Peasants, the majority of China's population at the time, were certainly ecstatic; however, later through the continuing series of 'classicide' and land reform policies, the communist government could nationalize any land they want, becoming the real beneficiary of the land reform. After Deng's economic reform and during the bubble, selling land to developers became a fruitful approach for government earnings. This fashion of acquiring revenue has gone out of control due to the lack of supervision and experience, and the government itself paved the road of the housing bubble, nationalizing land for profit and trade them at higher and higher prices. For Chinese citizens, access to foreign investments are rather restricted compared to that of the citizens of most countries, which made purchasing domestic properties become the most desirable option for asset preservation and appreciation. After trillions of dollars were lost due to the Chinese stock market crash in 2015, the central bank started to encourage potential equity investors. Ever since that, the Chinese have historically invested much more of their money in properties than in the financial markets. Social reasons are also critical contributors to China's housing bubble, as some of the country's traditional value is having sparks with the values of modern society. For example, owning a property has become an important requirement for Chinese men when Chinese women are seeking for a husband. In fact, asking your date whether he owns a place to live or not has become a somewhat expected question in a family or friend arranged blind date. This kind of cultural pressure has pushed buying a property to become a slightly abnormal yet essential necessity for Chinese citizens, contributing to China's increasing housing prices. Another vital social contributor to the housing bubble is the Hukou system. As mentioned previously, a person's hukou not only limits the education resource he or she has access to but also the employment opportunities, medical resources, and other welfare provisions. Important resources on par with Western standards are only available in tier-one cities such as Beijing and

Shanghai, which has made the populace among small cities and rural areas considerably disadvantaged, causing massive migration to big cities. To understand how much welfare and benefits come with a hukou in tier-one cities, the Chinese often quantify a hukou's value to real money; it is commonly acknowledged that having a residency in a tier-one city is the equivalent of having hundreds of thousands of RMB and a much brighter future for one and his or her offspring compared to those who have their hukou in small cities.

For now, as there are signs and data are showing that China's property market is about to enter a time of recession comparing to previous times, the central banks are 'pumping' more and more money, and policymakers are struggling to stimulate the market. Nevertheless, the problem is deep-rooted; incentivizing policies and giving out loans are only temporary solutions to stall the oncoming crash. The burst of China's housing market is inevitable, and it is getting closer and closer as the country's economic growth is slowing down by other causes also. When the bubble does burst, although there is a slight difference between China's property market and that of the US, an economic crisis is imminent.

THE BYGONE LABOR ADVANTAGE

A significant advantage of China's tremendous growth is its massive and cheap labor, however, as the economy thrives, the country's labor force is no longer cheap due to the increasing necessitate for higher salaries and better working environment.

Despite China's opening-up policy, the Chinese market is still somewhat restrictive in terms of foreign direct investment (FDI); the real attraction to FDI is its labor, and besides this, China does not have any apparent advantages compare to other countries. China's labor advantage is no longer in existence.

In the late 2000s, the Chinese government introduced a new labor law which raised the pay for workers and widened their rights. The new labor law certainly provides further protection to worker's right and offers more comfortable working conditions; however, this policy also brought downsides to the country's economy. The cost to keep labor force were on the rise, and it became more challenging to employ temporary workers, therefore, those manufacturers with lower margins and exporters that tended to have order fluctuations started to withdraw from China since having a factory in China was no longer financially logical. In fact, many countries in Southeast Asia have even cheaper labor cost, and China's new labor law made many foreign investors realized that. After the implementation of the law, big foreign manufacturers started to exit China and to move their production to countries like Bangladesh, Vietnam, and Sri Lanka, in order to cut costs. The law and China's improved living standards resulted in a large number of factory closures since the introduction, which ultimately became a negative factor in the country's economic growth. Another predicament of China's present labor force is that the majority of the laborers are only 'day to day' laborers who do not possess any advanced skills, and as technology develops, unskilled workers are becoming more and more obsolete. The previous success of China's economy was mostly its production industry, which only offered the basic works to the laborers such as making clothes and packing things. This scarcity of skilled workers languishes China's progress to a more advanced level of manufacturing, such as automobile production. Have you ever seen a Chinese car outside of China? Probably not. If you are an iPhone user, you have probably noticed on the back of your iPhone that they are only assembled in China, not made in China, and they are designed in California. China's economy was not based upon the abilities of the workers but the inexpensive price. While the labor cost rises, China's FDI market is no longer dependable. If the status quo cannot be changed as the Chinese government is unable to level up the quality of its labor force, the entire Chinese economy will be affected negatively.

CHINESE EXPORTS ARE TUMBLING

A direct result of China's loss of its labor advantage is China's plummeting exports. China was once called the 'World Factory,' and exports were always an important portion of the country's economic growth since the beginning of this century. However, with the unchecked currency inflation occurring in the past decades, the cost of living in China has skyrocketed, and the country is now gradually losing its competitiveness.

China's exports growth has been gradually falling in recent years, and the election of Donald Trump is not making things better for China. China has always been a must-attack target for every US president since the 21st century, and Trump's tariffs are becoming the biggest hit on the Chinese economy. In addition to the already treacherous situation of China's economy, tariffs could make China's export growth plunge to low single digits and perhaps the negative region.

Although the percentage of export in China's GDP growth is trending downward as the government is obviously attempting to transfer its export-led economy to a consumption-economy like that of the US, the country's GDP growth is also projected lower than before in recent years. The escalated cost of living in China is preventing the transition from happening. What's even worse is that the abysmal living cost has led to a skyrocketing household debt. As of 2018, the country's ratio of household debt to its GDP has hit an all-time high of 50.3 percent, showing no signs of slowing down. As China's household debt keeps climbing, a portion of the consumer's income would have to go to interest payment, which indicates a negative effect on the consumer's purchasing power thus less consumption growth. It seems rather impossible for the Chinese government to transfer its economy to a consumption-led one in the short term, at least not without pains. Most importantly, China's tumbling exports are already hurting its economy.

A SLOWING ECONOMY

China's economy is slowing down, and the growth rate might just decline even more. China emerged as a miracle of economic development; however, its GDP growth rate is not as fierce as before, even the Chinese government itself has started to cut its growth target. To give you a general outlook of the contrast between the target growth by the Chinese government and the real GDP growth of the last decade, I created the following graph according to the data which I retrieved from the National Bureau of Statistics of China and the World Bank.

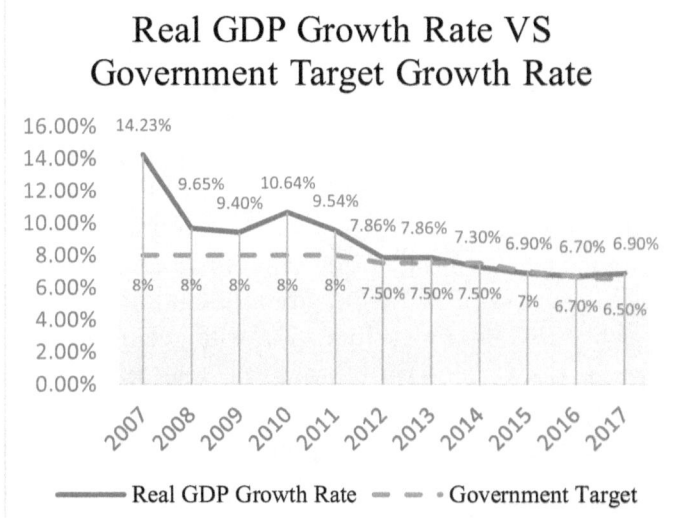

Real GDP Growth Rate VS Government Target Growth Rate

As we can see from the figure above, the Chinese government cut the target growth rate in 2012 for the first time in many years. Since then, the real GDP of China each year has not exceeded the target GDP by more than one percent like before. Again, I am not one of those pessimists who has been saying that China's economy is a giant bubble and it will soon collapse, however, I do believe that the acceleration of China's economic growth has already peaked, what we will see in the next decades is a continuous declining growth rate going towards a stable 2% per year, if nothing unexpected should happen. As the country slowly becomes a more developed country, China can no longer grow as rapidly as it did before. If China's GDP growth did not slow down and there were no target cuts with an annual GDP growth rate of 6.5%, the country would undoubtedly be a potential threat to the United States which, as of now, only has a GDP growth rate of 2% per year. Let us also not forget that GDP is not the only factor that measures the economic power and development; compared with average Americans, the majority of the people in China are rather destitute as before, in terms of purchasing power parity (PPP) per capita with the adjustments of price differences. The affluence of a nation or government does not mean that the people of the nation are affluent and enjoying their lives, while a wealthy nation with relatively poor citizens does not constitute as a real prosperous country, and such country is not fit for a power race; the collapse of the Soviet Union serves as an example.

THE CHINESE WAYS OF CORRUPTION

A relatively clean and uncorrupted government has always been one of the key contributors to a strong nation. The corruption in the Chinese government is much more severe than those of the Western world. Since the Chinese government is controlled by only one party, the country is arguably destined to have serious corruption problems. Along with the single-party system, Chinese culture itself also facilitates the large corruption problem in the country. Although China does not have an official or major religion that has an irrepressible presence, the ideologies of Confucianism are heavily ingrained in the minds of Chinese people, melted into traditional Chinese culture, affecting people's way of thinking and actions, and some of the creeds in Confucianism actually encourage bribery among officials. Anti-corruption has been one of the biggest tasks for the Chinese government since Xi Jinping took office, while the country is showing a declining growth, corruption still remains as a considerable obstacle that keeps China a politically anemic country unless China changes its political party system, or, start another cultural revolution that expunges the pedantic beliefs in the traditional culture, and both of the solutions seem impossible considering the current political and social climate of China.

A country controlled by only one political party means that there are at least these three deflects that are unavoidable when it comes to government structure and bureaucracy. First of all, the lack of supervision, is the primary problem of a single-party government. When there is only one party in the government, it has no competition or rivalry that has the desire or power to bring down the ruling party; this has been the case since 1949 when the Chinese Communist Party (CCP) officially established control in mainland China. While there are no other parties that can monitor the behaviors of the members and officials of the ruling party, what is going on inside the government is unclear to the people, which brings us the second problem of a single-party system, the lack of transparency. Transparency and clarity are the cornerstone of a mature government with little or zero corruption, however, without the supervision from the opposite party, there are no ways for the public to find out what happened and how things happened; bribery and malfeasance happen freely among government officials. In an authoritarian regime like China, the media is often controlled by the government, so is the news about the government itself, therefore, the public can only read whatever the government allows you to read. To such a degree, every single form of media covered or related to the government is ultimately biased and lack objectiveness, which is the third defect of a single-party system. All of these problems contribute to the corruption, with the Chinese communist government not willing to give up its dictatorial power, this dilemma might just exist everlasting until the system changes.

On a related note, the top leadership of the Chinese communist government has been attempting to crack down corruption, however, eliminating corruption also became a tool of political strife inside the party to eradicate potential opponents. In fact, cleansing oppositions played a much bigger role than actually cracking down corruption in the entire anti-corruption campaign under Xi Jinping. The concept of 'factional struggle' is not new to those who pay close attention to the infighting of Chinese Communist Party, and Xi took the fight to a new level with his anti-corruption campaign, breaking the unspoken tradition of the "implicit impunity" for Politburo Standing Committee members (刑不上常

委) which consist of the highest leadership of the CCP. While bringing down his fellow comrades like Bo Xilai, Zhou Yongkang, and Former PLA General Xu Caihou in the name of anti-corruption, Xi and his campaign remind me of Joseph Stalin and his Great Purge.

Another contributor to China's corruption problem, the combination of some of the most pedantic ideologies of Confucianism and traditional Chinese culture, has been a hidden element that people often neglect when studying corruption in China. Confucianism, as a philosophy and a 'rationalistic religion', continued to develop and spread for over thousands of years, with its Four Books and Five Classics (四書五經) which serve as the foundation and essence of the belief. Among the Five Classics, Liji (禮記), or the Classic of Rites, lay at the nucleus of the Confucian canon. Deeply interconnected with the way that Chinese think and act, some doctrines in the book are well memorized and deeply ingrained in almost every single literate Chinese. For instance, in the first chapter of the book, Quli, or the Summary of the Rules of Propriety, translated by Scottish sinologist James Legge,

禮尚往來。往而不來，非禮也；來而不往，亦非禮也。

And what the rules of propriety value is that reciprocity. If I give a gift and nothing comes in return, that is contrary to propriety.

The first sentence, which can be seen as an idiom, is one of those terms that every Chinese family knows. Instead of remembering that bribery is illegal, the Chinese would rather continue to believe the concept of 'Propriety suggests reciprocity'. One has to bring and give if one has a favor to ask, and in the case of Chinese culture, there is no favor, only reciprocity. Powerful officials would not help you if you cannot bring benefits to the executor, and the people who need help would not expect the authorities to deliver if he or she does not bring in valuable gifts, which eventually formed a vicious circle in not only the government but also the entire society. In a hospital, if a patient is to have a surgery, the family of the patient often give a relatively large amount of money to the surgeon, beyond the required payment, in the form of 'Red Pockets,' even if doing the surgery is their job. Although it is clearly stated in the law that bribery is unlawful, giving and accepting money in exchange of doing a 'favor' has become a social norm among Chinese people, making the country's corruption problem even worse.

Corruption does not make a country stronger; it only weakens the country. In the case of China, perhaps until the change of regime, corruption will always remain as a huge factor that is negatively influencing China's economy.

DROPPING POPULATION

Population has always been one of the most important factors that determine the strength and potential of a country, and China has been the most populated country on this planet for centuries. Higher population is often seen as an advantage in most scenarios, especially in the case when the land size of the country is large enough to allocate the resources in a less stressful manner. The enormous population of China, often considered as the biggest advantage of China and a threat to the Western world, is now dwindling. India will surpass China in terms of population promptly, and China itself is actually facing a population crisis. From the 1980s to the 2000s, in less than one generation, the newborn population of China has shrunk more than 30%. The birth rate of China's population has decreased from 1987's 23.33% to 2017's 12.43%, while the death rate climbed from 6.72% to 7.11% in the same period. From a macro-perspective, the percentage of the Chinese population of the whole world was once over 30% in the 19th century and over 25 % in the 20th century, and now its population only represents less than 20% of the world's population. Mostly because of China's One-Child Policy and the younger generation's change of view on having babies and getting married, China is now among the countries with the lowest fertility rate, and the number is projected to go even lower in the near future. The replacement of the One-Child Policy with the Two-Child Policy seemed rather futile to reverse the trend of lower and lower birthrate; China is losing its most significant advantage, more importantly, the population of China is facing a potential collapse.

Before the implementation of the One-Child Policy, China had a robust birthrate that is higher than the world average at that time. There were more middle-aged men and women than children and senior citizens. Presently, although there are fewer and fewer children being born each year, the population of children still remains higher than that of seniors. However, the growth rate of the population is distinctly declining. The math is simple. In about a decade, the growth rate of the population will be negative. Unless the birthrate can be brought back up to the world average, China's population decline will be unstoppable, and the result of which is unimaginable.

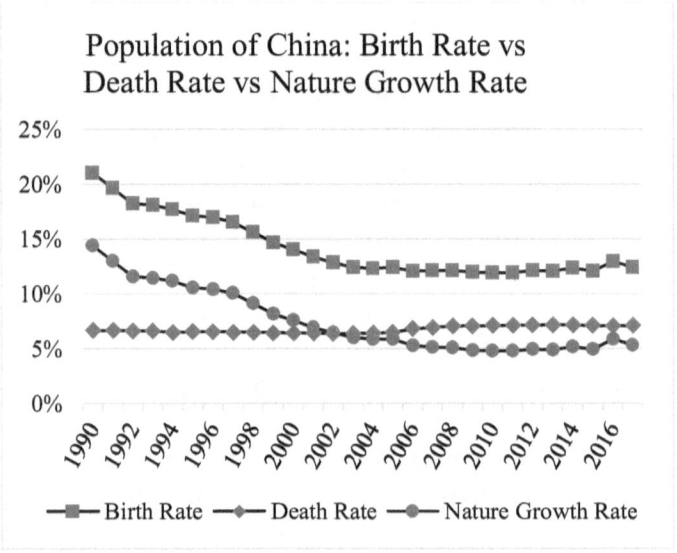

Population of China: Birth Rate vs Death Rate vs Nature Growth Rate

In 2016, China lifted its ban on its citizens for having more than one child, aiming to alleviate the potential crisis. Nevertheless, the effort appeared to be rather unavailing. Because of the long-suppressed desire of producing a second child finally being released, the number of newborns in 2016 was clearly higher than that of 2015, and the birth rate was expected to peak in 2017. 2017 was also commonly expected to be the year with the most newborns. However, the total population of Chinese newborns of 2017 was even less than that of 2016, by more than half a million. The number of this so-called peak year of newborns is much less than the number of newborns at the end of the 1980s, due to the inordinately low birthrate. As seen on the figure above, the birthrate dropped just one year after nullifying the One-Child policy.

There are also other predicaments brought on by the low fertility rate. For example, the current population of China is aging faster than ever. As a consequence of fewer and fewer children being born, the proportion of senior citizens in the total population is rising quickly, and China's improvement of life expectancy is making the case worse. In 2016, there were over 200 million Chinese citizens who were older than 60, representing approximately 17 % of its total population, and this is only the beginning of a fast-aging population with less and less newborns.

China did not shake the burden off after opening the Two-Child policy. In fact, the demographic crisis could be severer than any other problems that China is facing. Perhaps, it is fair to say that China has already lost its most significant advantage. The status quo and future projection of China's demography indicate that China's economic growth will be affected and limited, and such an important factor should be counted and carefully considered when predicting China's future development and economic growth.

A chapter, or even a whole book, is never comprehensive enough to cover all the problems and instabilities of China's economy and society. However, with what is there, it is certain that the economy of China does not have the capacity to outpace the US, nor do the many problems of its society allow the country to be perceived as a formidable threat. Instead, what's waiting ahead of China is going to be years of fixing its current issues and spending much on maintaining its social stability, if the country does not collapse itself. For the purpose of reminding both me and the readers, the followings are the primary problems I surveyed above and some other secondary challenges that China is facing which were not addressed in this chapter.

- Unequal Education: Education is the essence of human civilization. Having a fine and well-balanced education system is the intrinsic solution to social insecurity. China is far from achieving that goal.
- Housing Market Bubble: China's economy might not be in a bubble, but its property market certainly is, and if the bubble does burst, the damage to the entire economy of China is unimaginable. More and more signs of an upcoming explosion of the Chinese housing market are emerging as the central government is running out of means to regulate this very section.

- The Plunging Export: China was, and it still is an export-oriented country. Despite that the country has started the attempt to transition itself into a consumption-based economy, the many other instabilities that come with it are preventing a successful transformation from happening. Donald Trump's extreme tariffs on China's exports are further damaging the country's already tumbling exports and its economy.

- China's Labor Advantage is Obsolete: Once making China's economy take off, labor in China is no longer cheap. China's labor force has failed to become competent. FDI in China is getting lower and lower as the country is struggling to improve the quality of its labor force.

- Ineradicable Corruption: Corruption in China is partially rooted in its culture. Most importantly, the one-party controlled government is the origin of corruption. The lack of transparency and supervision cannot be solved because of the system. Since the communist government does not welcome a change of system, the country's economy will always be haunted by corruption.

- The Weakening Population of China: Although China still has the largest population in the world (at the moment of writing this), the country is facing a potential crisis that its population is not only dropping but also aging. China is about to lose its most prominent advantage of prospering.

- Pollution: Yes, almost all the developed countries went through a phase of enduring horrible pollution. However, China, as the largest newly industrialized country, seemingly has no luxury of halting the pollution if the Chinese government wishes to keep the economy growing. As a result, the pollution in China, including air pollution, water pollution, industrial waste, and soil contamination, has caused serious environmental and health issues.
- Ethnic Conflict (human rights violations): As one of the largest multinational states, China is having a hard time mediating religious and ethnic conflict. Using armed forces and labor camps to repress the Uyghurs and the Tibetans are neither ethical nor permanent solutions to keep the society stable.

CHAPTER III

THE CHINESE MILITARY: WEAKER THAN YOU THINK & INADQUATE FOR A CONFLICT

Yes, the Chinese has the largest army in the world. Yes, the Chinese are increasing their defense budgets. And yes, the Chinese are crossing lines in the South China Sea. However, none of these statements guarantee that China will be victorious if the country is to have an armed conflict even with its surrounding neighbors due to its seemingly powerful military but verily inadequate and the containment in the Asia-Pacific region by the United States with its island chains and allies. In addition to the unwarlike nature of the Chinese people and its foreign policy, this chapter explains why the Chinese military is not as powerful as you think and why China should not be considered a threat to security.

FROM RECRUITING TO FIGHTING: THE PROBLEMS WITH CHINESE MILITARY

We all have seen how strong and well-trained the soldiers are in the US military, and we would expect the same from other soldiers around the world. However, China is a different story. As you have probably observed, many of the Chinese international students tend to need glasses as a result of genetic and environmental causes, the phenomenon is the same in China; almost 9 in 10 Chinese youngsters suffer from near-sightedness, and 37% of the population wear glasses in some large Chinese cities. Along with other requirements, a good vision is certainly a vital necessity for a soldier. However, in China, the recruitment officers are seeing a significant downturn in the physical healthiness of candidates; more and more are considered unfit because of myopia and weight problems. Before the adjustments of standards for physical fitness, over 23 percent of the applicants failed the vision test, and around 20 percent of them were either overweight or too light to join the military; the situation led to two drops of standards for physical fitness in the past years. The physical condition of soldiers in the military might not be the ultimate deciding factor in a conflict, but it is inarguably the most fundamental component of a strong military.

What would be the training regime for soldiers once they joined the military? One would expect that the most of a soldier's time allocation should be dedicated to training to become a warrior; nevertheless, the case is again different in the Chinese military.

For the Chinese military, another priority of training its soldiers is to achieve the political and ideological indoctrination. The People's Liberation Army (PLA) requires its soldiers to dedicate at least 20 to 30 percent of their time to political and ideological studies on Chinese Communism and leadership, and the allotment would rise to 40 percent during induction training, according to the research scientist at the Center for Naval Analyses. The guidelines for Chinese military training given by the Ministry of Education is to 'promote patriotism, collectivism, and revolutionary heroism.' Why are the PLA soldiers required to devote such a large portion of their training time to study party doctrines? That is because the PLA does not belong to the People's Republic of China; it belongs to the Communist Party of China. If the PLA soldiers are going to war, they are not fighting for the country; instead, they are fighting for the party. If China is invaded, the PLA soldiers are not responsible for protecting the country but only to protect the party. The communist party has the absolute control over the PLA, and the Commander in Chief of the PLA is often the General Secretary of the Communist Party of China, therefore, the Ministry of National Defense, surprisingly, has no control over the PLA, while the Central Military Commission (CMC) is the unconditional authority. The PLA in China would be equivalent to an army controlled by the Democratic party or the Republican party in the US, not by the nation nor by the people, which is also why the Chinese soldiers are required to devote that much of their training time to study party ideologies; after all, brainwashing is essential to eliminate disloyalty.

In addition to the training time dedicated to study and restudy the political doctrines, there are also other 'futile' practices and activities that occupy a certain percentage of soldier's training time. For instance, my high school is one of those institutions that require the newly admitted freshmen to participate a seven days or longer mandatory military training, for the purposes of learning military disciplines, better understanding Communist ideologies, and to better prepare for the hard work in higher-level education. I could not and should not recall the type and name of the PLA platoon that trained us, however, I clearly remember that the officer who supervised my class told us that not folding your bed sheet correctly disqualify one's ability as a soldier, and we would spend hours every day on studying and practicing how to make the perfect fold that looks like a squared tofu, and the shape and steadiness of our folded blanket were taken into account of our daily performance. Other stuff we had to learn and practice every day include how to clap correctly and uniformly after the superiors finished talking, how to sit while listening to the superiors, and how to do goose steps. If a military indeed spends most of its training time on ideologies and folding blankets, it means the military is probably

66

not combat ready, and it is certainly not preparing for an armed conflict at all.

The equipment of the soldiers is exceptionally crucial in any military operations; a better and more advanced set of equipment can not only save the soldier's life but also assist the solider to eliminate enemy forces. Although China is second in the defense budget and military spending with over 200 billion dollars, the country is not spending much on equipping its soldiers. Adding even the raincoat and saddle into the equipment expenditure, it takes less than 9,500 RMB, approximately 1500 USD to equip a Chinese soldier, while half of the cost comes from the most basic equipment of a soldier, a rifle. The Type 95 automatic rifle, valuing 4,300 RMB, is the most expensive piece of equipment on a Chinese soldier, while the combat helmet comes the second, costing around 1580 RMB, and no bulletproof armor is equipped. In comparison, the equipment of each US soldier cost around 17,500 USD, with the advanced armor and other high-tech protections, and this was in 2007. The cost of a Chinese soldier's equipment is about the equivalent to the cost of a US soldier's gears in the 1970s, around 50 years ago; If China and the US are to meet each other in a conflict, for the PLA, it would be considered as fighting an advanced army from the future; what are the chances of losing a battle for a military that is half a century behind in gear?

One may ask where all the military budget went if equipping a Chinese soldier is this cheap, the answer is that a large portion of the spending is allocated on reconfiguring the outdated, yet still-in-use equipment and weapons and repairing the obsolete weapons that could hurt the soldiers who use them. Perhaps because of the fast-growing economy of China for the past decades, Chinese people's lives have gotten better while its soldiers have also grown bigger in size, which made them no longer fit in their own tanks. As reported by the Chinese military's General Armament Department, the average height of the PLA soldiers had increased by 2 cm (approximately 0.8 inches), and the waist girth had risen by 5 cm (approximately 1.5 inches), after conducting the survey on around 20,000 Chinese soldiers. Such an enlargement of physiques indicates the tanks that were produced and designed decades ago have become awfully congested for the current soldiers, and the shoulder stocks of rifles are no longer long enough for these soldiers, affecting the weapon's accuracy and usability. On the other hand, after surveying over 3,000 US soldiers and national guards, a study found that the height of today's US military men did not change much at all compared to physiques of the soldiers in 1988. Very simple math here, the US military does not need to spend much on reconfiguring its equipment, thus more spending on research and development, forming a virtuous circle in terms of advancing the equipment. Antithetically, many of the Chinese soldiers are in danger of using outworn equipment and gears, further falling behind with the militaries of Western nations.

Some say that the level of equipment and soldier quality is not the unconditional factor that decides the victorious side in a war; assuredly, the battlefield experience of soldiers and a seamless joint-command system are also crucial elements in winning a conflict; however, the PLA has neither of those. The last time China had an actual armed conflict with another country would be the Sino-Vietnamese War in 1979, a short border warfare ended with both sides declaring victory, while the majority of Western scholars concur that the Vietnamese military outmatched the PLA due to the Chinese withdrawal from the country and Vietnam's continued occupation of Cambodia until ten years later. Lasting less than one month, this conflict is practically the only battlefield experience that the PLA ever had in 40 years, and the soldiers who participated in the warfare are either deceased or retired. As for the last time that the PLA was massively deployed on the ground, it was in 1989, at Tiananmen Square, oppressing the country's very own students and workers. Other than the Sino-Vietnamese War in 1979 and some minor operations against terrorist and pirates, the only few shows of force by the PLA are at its anniversary parades. On the other side of the ocean, the US has been involved continuously in all different types of wars since the beginning of the 20th century, from the First World War to Operation Freedom's Sentinel (War in Afghanistan). The conflicts involving the US are much more than just regular on-ground battles; airstrikes, drone strikes, naval bombardment, cyber-attacks, and many other advanced manners of combat operations that are performed to achieve its goals. Although the fact that the US has been consistently involved in conflicts is not fortunate for everyone, these warfare experiences made sure that the US military, along with its vigorous Western allies, is always combat ready.

Development and technology not only changed our lives but also changed the ways of fighting a war. Ever since World War II, countries have witnessed the power of joint operations. Nazi Germany allegedly created the world's first joint command system during the World War II, Oberkommando der Wehrmacht (The Upper Command of Armed Forces), oversighting its navy, army and air force. With the joint command structure, Nazi Germany formed their notorious Blitzkrieg (lightning assault) way of attack, quickly and successfully invaded Poland and France. The ODW showed the world the power and efficiency of combining forces together for military operations. Modern warfare can no longer be fought without forces working jointly under one command. Under the Department of Defense, the US Joint Chiefs of Staff regard joint warfare as the most fundamental doctrine of the armed forces, calling it a 'team warfare.' The joint command system has been the reason for many successful military operations; the importance of having an established joint command structure is evident. Notwithstanding, China, as the second in defense spending in the world, only recently created their supposedly functioning joint command system, the Joint Staff Department of the Central Military Commission, in 2016, under Xi's new reform. In addition, around 70 percent of the PLA soldiers belong to the PLA Army, and almost all senior officers on the Central Military Commission are army officers, which could be a serious difficulty for the newly formed Joint Staff

Department when it comes to decision-making time involving naval and aerial affairs. In any case, if the CMC wishes to make China's new joint command system functional, there is still a long way to go to remedy the virtually zero experience of operation and other difficulties. Compared to the US and its Western allies, China's joint force structure seems rather futile and fragile than threatening.

As mentioned previously, the single-party system made corruption one of the most exhausting problems for the Chinese government to counter. The problem extended beyond the government body; the corruption and malfeasance in the PLA are worse than one can imagine. As a party-controlled military in a single-party administrated country, the PLA is utterly immune to external supervision, with no budgetary transparency and zero responsibility to the government for how and how much it spends the country's capital and resources. To understand the severity of corruption in PLA, simply look at the high-ranking military officials who were arrested since the beginning of the 21st century. In 2000, Ji Shengde, former Chief of Military Intelligence in the PLA's General Staff Department, was arrested and sentenced to death for selling information and corruption; Gu Junshan, former Deputy Director of the PLA General Logistics Department (GLD) and former Chief of Housing Division of the GLD, who reportedly owned several stashes of gold and dozens of properties each with an area over 1,800 sq. ft. around the Second Ring Road of Beijing's inner city, was charged with bribery and embezzlement, and he was sentenced to death with a two-year-reprieve in

2015; linked with Gu, Xu Caihou, the former Vice Chairman of the Central Military Commission and former member of the Politburo of the Communist Party of China, was detained and under investigation until he died of bladder cancer in prison. Along with Xu, another former co-Vice Chairman of the CMC and former member of the Politburo, General Guo Boxiong was charged with bribery and sentenced to life imprisonment. Other than accepting bribes from non-military personnel, it is believed that the higher-ranking officers often take bribes from lower-ranking officers in exchange of promotions or certain positions. In PLA, it seems like the time in service and performance are not the only and necessary factors for a promotion; the ability to take bribes from others and give some of that gain to a superior became another way of advancing upward in the military. It is widely believed that the degree of corruption is sometimes minimalized when the government announced the numbers, and many corruption cases are reported to the public with no numbers due to the substantial amount of money involved in the bribery, for the sake of not 'alerting' the public; much of the military money privatized by the officials are counted towards the defense budget, which further empties the meaning of China's position of second in defense spending in the world. Following is an example of how corrupted of a military official can be.

Former Deputy Director of GLD Gu Junshan's
Mansion in Puyang, Henan.

It is not hard to picture the level of corruption in the
other ranks when the Generals (highest rank in PLA)
of a military are imprisoned for life. Among the lower
tiers, there are other forms of malfeasances and
corruption existing. Mid-level ranking PLA officers
would privatize their military-assigned houses and
properties and list them on the open market either
for sale or rent, which is completely illegal. Because
of the policy that police cannot write tickets to
vehicles with military plates, lower ranking personnel
often install the military plates on their own vehicles,
and they can park wherever they wish, speed above
limits, and avoid all tolls. Corruption is a colossal
problem in the PLA; however, the bigger problem is
that there has not been any effective way to solve and
prevent the problems from happening, again, unless
China changes its political system. Regardless of the
ways of solving the dilemma, a heavily corrupted
military will collapse itself before its foes.

Isolated: Lack of Allies

From the recent activities around the South China Sea and the East China Sea during the past decade, it is undeniable that China is aiming for regional hegemony. However, with the strategic shift of the US from the Middle East to the Asia-Pacific and the military development of China's neighboring countries, it becomes harder and harder for China to make any attempts militarily.

First of all, China has no 'allies.' By no 'allies,' I mean that China does not have a true ally that can provide military support or any other form of assistance if China is to be involved in a war. Let us look at the No.1 supposable 'ally' that people often link with China, North Korea. There is no doubt that China and North Korea were in a firm alliance during the Korean War. However, that was over 60 years ago. The China-North Korean relationship has been declining gradually since the beginning of the 21st century after the North Koreans started to conduct their nuclear tests, while there is no official declaration confirming China and North Korea is in a military alliance. China has always been an opponent of North Korea's nuclear tests, but both of Kim's administrations acted indifferent toward China's opinion on this matter. China, as a participant in the Six-Party Talks that aims to resolve the problems of North Korea's nuclear weapons, pressured North Korea many times to give up its program, eventually started to support sanctions against North Korea, which led to a serious deterioration of the relationship between the two countries. In 2017, the

74

state news agency of North Korea, Korean Central News Agency (KCNA), unprecedentedly criticized China, accusing China of "big-power chauvinism", claiming that "The Democratic People's Republic of Korea will never beg for the maintenance of friendship with China", after China banned its imports of coal from North Korea. Other than the disagreement over the issues of the nuclear program, the incidents of North Korean's impoundment of Chinese fishing boats have always been a huge factor that is worsening the Sino-North Korean relationship. You would think the communist neighbors could efficiently resolve a miniature issue like this; however, these incidents often end up with North Koreans asking for higher and higher ransoms in order to release the captured Chinese fishermen. Although China still remains as North Korea's closest 'friend', calling the Sino-North Korean relationship as an alliance is rather farfetched. It appears that China and North Korea are only cooperating to prevent the US and South Korean invasion to the North; China is an ally of North Korea only if Washington is to attack North Korea, while North Korea just remains as China's communist neighbor whose only benefit to China is to serve as the buffer zone between China and the powers on the side of the US.

The other commonly believed ally of China, Pakistan, though different from North Korea and having a much better relationship with China, is not a capable power that can provide support to China other than backing the country up diplomatically, except in a situation that involves India and its territory. First and foremost, Pakistan itself is often in an economic crisis, and it is still in one; the developing nation is having trouble to lift itself out of a financial crisis, not to mention providing aid to other countries. In 2008, Pakistan's inflation rate skyrocketed to 25%, facing a serious bankruptcy situation. A decade later, in the first half of the year, Pakistan had a current account deficit of $18 billion, representing roughly 45 percent increment from last year's account deficit of $12.4 billion, while its foreign-exchange reserves could only cover the imports for less than two months, driving Pakistan into another financial crisis. Although China is always there to help Pakistan's economy to get back on the right track, the fact that China is investing more and more in the country also substantiates Pakistan's inability to aid China economically. A package from the International Monetary Fund (IMF) is an option for Pakistan, however, due to the nation's relationship with China, the US is highly unlikely to give the pass to Pakistan.

In terms of military development, the Pakistan Armed Forces are growing rapidly due to the rivalry with its Indian neighbor, maintaining a close relationship with the PLA. Nevertheless, there is hardly anything that Pakistan can do to help China. Despite the fact that Pakistan borders the Arabian Sea, it is practically impossible for its navy to reach the areas of potential conflict for China. In order to get to the South China Sea, Pakistan will have to go through the obstacles of India, Sri Lanka, perhaps Malay and Indonesia's Malacca Strait, and eventually the potential foes of China, i.e. Vietnam. No matter how durable the Pakistan military is, it is difficult for the country to serve the role of an ally of China in the Asia-Pacific region.

In addition, there is one thing that has often been ignored by many experts in the world; Chinese government's constant oppression of Muslim and Xinjiang Uyghurs could potentially sabotage the good relationship between China and Pakistan. Currently, the Pakistani government are showing the two countries' strong relationship and praising the good of China to its people mostly because of the substantial amount of support and continuous aid from China. If a change of regime that values more on its Islamic culture in Pakistan and a switch of attitude and policy toward Pakistan from India happens, the Sino-Pakistani tie could be weakened due to China's treatment on its Muslim population, thus breaking up the so-called military alliance.

CONTAINED: BY THE ISLANDS CHAINS

While the two supposed allies of China might not be able to perform their duties as allies, the United States and its allies are containing China's military growth and influence successfully. Although the US often denies its containment policy of China, the actions and focuses on military development of the US and its four powerful allies in the Asia-Pacific region are proving otherwise.

A friend of mine who is an enthusiast of history and politics once asked me how many aircraft carriers the US has, and I answered 20---confidently. He said "wrong". I then asked him for the correct answer. "21.

People always forget about the largest aircraft carrier that the US has, and that is Japan," he answered with a smirk on his face. Of course, he was joking. However, the joke has its logic behind it. Japan, as one of the largest major non-NATO allies of the US, certainly provide much more than what an aircraft carrier can give, and it plays the principle role in containing China. As one of the nations that are holding the first islands chain to contain China, Japan utilized the Senkaku Islands (尖閣諸島) or Diaoyu Islands (钓鱼岛) in Chinese as the critical point to limit and test China's action, and it has been successful by far. With a combined area of less than 3 square miles and no one populating the islands, this group of islands has been in dispute between China and Japan for over 40 years since China started to claim its sovereignty over these islands after the pass of the Okinawa Reversion Agreement by the US Senate which acknowledges that the Senkaku Islands should return to Japan in 1972. If China gains the administration of the Diaoyu Islands, the first island chain would be easily broken through as the islands are located to the south of Japan's Okinawa Prefecture and north of Taiwan, and China, very possibly, will reclaim the lands, which would be the last thing Japan wants to see. However, the dispute has been in existence for over four decades now, although there have been attempts from China of taking over the islands, the status quo remains precisely the same as half of a century ago---Japan having more control of the Senkaku Islands, symbolizing the success of the China containment policy by the US and Japan. In addition to the aircraft carrier joke, while Japan already has four aircraft carriers, China, as one of the members of the United Nation Security Council, has only recently tested its first aircraft carrier built domestically, not to mention the PLA Navy's first aircraft carrier, Liaoning, was an abandoned Soviet-Era aircraft carrier that was purchased from Ukraine as a training ship which reportedly had to return to the port immediately due to an engine failure during a sea trial. On the opposite side, compared to any of the US's nuclear-powered supercarriers, neither the Liaoning aircraft carrier nor China's current home-constructing Type 001A are a match.

The international community is not comfortable with China's military action either, which further assists the containment strategy led by the US. China's Nine-Dash Line, a demarcation line, initially published by the Republic of China (Taiwan) and later adopted by both China and Taiwan after the Chinese Civil War, encompasses the majority of the South China Sea, which includes many disputed Islands that China is not in control of (Notice that the Nine-Dash Line claim is not a product of today's China and its fast-growing economy and military, it was brought up before the founding of People's Republic of China). The dispute over Scarborough Shoal (黄岩岛) between China and the Philippines quickly escalated to a standoff, with battleships from both sides patrolling around the area and getting ready for a conflict. In the beginning of 2013, with the support from the international community, the Philippines officially filed the arbitration case against China's action and claim on the areas enclosed in

China's so-called Nine-Dash Line which entails both the disputed Spratly Islands with Vietnam and Scarborough Shoal, indicating the illegality under the United Nations Convention on the Law of the Sea (UNCLOS). In 2016, the Permanent Court of Arbitration (PCA) tribunal in Netherland's Hague ruled unanimously in favor of the Philippines, concluding that there was no evidence indicating China's sole administration over these waters in history, thus it is illegitimate for China to claim historic rights over these territories (Notice that the decision made by the tribunal is ruled as final and not appealable by any countries). In addition to illegitimating China's claim, the PCA tribunal also indicates that China has violated the Philippines' sovereign rights in its Exclusive Economic Zone (EEZ). Although China rejected the results made by the Hague, this case showed the general attitude of the international community towards China's actions and claims, pressuring and preventing China from making any further moves, although the country's behavior was mainly trying to uphold its previous announcement (made before 1949) and not to lose any 'face' as a major power. While it is projected that the situation in the South China Sea will remain peaceful and unchanged, it is rather immature to categorize China as an expansionist since the country did not claim any extra territories outside of the Nine-Dash line.

In addition to the other neighbors of China, South Korea, although often not considered as a part of the first island chain, is a durable power that is maintaining the balance in East Asia. Although South

Korea is an Asian country, it shares more values with Western countries, which keeps the country on the side of the US; the ideology and system difference overshadows the close distance between China and South Korea geographically, making South Korea a willing country to balance China. Unlike Japan, South Korea is not bound by any self-defense laws that limit the type and size of its military. Due to the constant threat from the north and pressure from China, the South Koreans always regard military development as a top priority of the country. Despite the size of this peninsula nation, South Korea has a record of high military spending. In 2017, South Korea spent 39.2 billion USD on its military, ranking the 10th in the world. It is also stated in their constitution that South Korean men must fulfill years of military duty, which means almost half of the population is ready for combat if needed. With the support from the US and its military bases in the country, South Korea has been the key player in the success of containing China, and it will likely stay that way due to the continuing growth of the South Korean military and the rigid ideological difference between the two countries.

The US started to increase its presence and devote more energy to the Asia-Pacific region since the beginning of this century. Some call the strategical shift to Asia-Pacific 'too late' as they believe China has grown powerful enough to become a threat; however, the current situation and incidents proves that the increased American involvement is not only timely but also successful as of containing China. In East Asia, with the increased frequency of US-Japan, US-

South Korea joint military exercises implicate the resolute and powerful alliance between the US and its allies if any aggressive action should happen in the region, which indirectly prevent China from making any moves against the Senkaku Islands as mentioned above. An example of China not being able to act as a threat in these disputes is the lack of action taken on Socotra Rock which is also known as the Suyan Islet. Although the area is seen as disputed between China and South Korea, the South Korean government started construction on the rocks in the 1990s, representing a South Korean controlment over the territory, while all China could do was to protest in the silence. To the south of China, although the US is not allied with most of the nations in South East Asia, the increasing cooperation between the US and Association of Southeast Asian Nations (ASEAN) appears more and more similar to a military alliance with no written agreement. With one of the five key areas of US and ASEAN partnerships being 'expanding maritime cooperation,' other than providing economic and technological assistance, the US Mission to ASEAN clearly states that they are in support of 'the peaceful resolution of claims in the South China Sea in accordance with international law.' The defense ministers of ASEAN also decided to partner with the US for a military exercise in the South China Sea. Despite that ASEAN also had its computer-based drill with China, the operation was only aiming to practice search and rescue missions. This implies the contrast of the relationships between China and ASEAN and US and ASEAN. The upcoming US-ASEAN military exercise is believed to focus on the hypothetical conflicts that may take place in the disputed territories in the South China Sea, which could have the same effect as the military exercises conducted between the US and its allies in East Asia, further making China's Nine-Dash Line territory claim stays only as a claim.

As we see that China's military is unlikely to make any further moves in East and Southeast Asia due to the increased US presence and the islands chains, the country also faces strong constraint at its western border; India, now one of the fastest growing economies in the world, is not only balancing China's influence but also proving that China is not tough enough to be considered a threat as the border standoff that took place in Doklam shows. Doklam, which is actually not claimed by India, is a disputed area between China and India's ally Bhutan (Bhutan and India have a treaty which allows India to guide the country's foreign and defense affairs). China first sent construction teams to the area, and India quickly reacted with more troops and equipment to counter China's action. China then responded with threatening comments from its foreign ministry, demanding India to pull out its troops. With China as the seemingly much more powerful and richer country between these two, you would think China would take over the territory like Russia did to Crimea; however, the standoff lasted over two months and ended with Chinese withdrawal from Doklam. There are only two explanations of China's yield from Doklam. Firstly, the Chinese military is not as strong as it has presented to the world; China would not have withdrawn from the standoff if China is confident that the PLA is capable of winning the conflict, and China should understand the problems of its military better than anyone else does. Another explanation of China's unexpected withdrawal, which I believe is the ultimate explanation, is that China does not wish to start a conflict or another relentless dispute as it has with Japan over territory previously. Perhaps China backed away for both reasons, but there have been many signs that show China is rather peaceful and prefers to avoid conflicts, which we will discuss more in the following part. Although China has often been presented to the West as the initiator of regional disputes, China has actually resolved more conflicts than it has started in recent years; China has successfully resolved a whopping 17 out of 23 border disputes with other countries, and in most of these cases, China was often the one that made consequential concessions with the intent of reaching a settlement.

CHINA DOESN'T WANT A WAR

As previously mentioned in the first chapter, the Chinese are proven to have an unwarlike nature throughout the nation's history, although we cannot use a country's history to judge its current actions, China might be a different case. Some of the Western nations and those who share a different ideology with China's often view China as a dangerous adversary that is probably preparing for an invasive war. However, China's recent policy and actions are proving otherwise.

Speaking of a modern invasion, Weapons of Mass Destruction (WMD), although sounding dangerous and inhumane, would undoubtedly be a highly considerable option for an aggressive country. Reasonably, signing and ratifying the use of WMD treaties would suggest a country's positive attitude on banning the use and production of WMD, reflecting the country's proneness to peace. China has been an activist and forerunner on signing these treaties. As stated earlier, China is the only country among the five nuclear weapon states under the treaty on NPT that proclaimed and reaffirmed many times its policy of No First Use of nuclear weapons; in all scenarios, is it not a relief to know in advance that a state armed with nuclear weapons wouldn't use its most destructive weapon first? In addition to China's No First Use Policy, compared to the US' total of 1032 times of nuclear explosion tests, China has only conducted nuclear explosion tests less than 50 times, while both countries are the signatory of Comprehensive Nuclear-Test-Ban Treaty (CTBT). China has signed the Chemical Weapons Convention (CWC) and quickly ratified the treaty in the 1990s. As for biological weapons, China was among the world's biggest victims of large-scale biological warfare; during the Japanese occupation from 1937 to the end of World War II, the country was attacked, and its people were murdered by the biological weapons developed by the Japanese. It is estimated that over 500,000 were killed by Unit 731, a biological and chemical warfare research and development unit of the Imperial Japanese Army. The tragedy and suffering deeply influenced China's effort of nonproliferation; China has acceded to the Geneva

Protocol in 1952 and the Biological and Toxin Weapons Convention (BTWC) in 1984. World War II has traumatized the world, especially China which suffered thorough massive killings with unorthodox means. Today, from the perspective of WMD nonproliferation, it is safe to say that China does not want another war, at least not a conflict involving WMD.

Disarmament often represents a country's goal and effort to a peaceful development. Other than limiting and abolishing its WMD, China has been actively reducing the size of its military as well. Since the founding of the country in 1949, the PLA has reduced its troops over ten times. The major disarmaments are listed in the following table.

YEAR	TYPE OF DISARMAMENTS	NUMBERS
1950	Troop Reduction (After the Chinese Civil War, before the Korean War)	Approximately 5.5 million soldiers reduced to 4 million
1952	Troop Reduction (During the Korean War)	Approximately 6.1 million soldiers reduced to 4.2 million
1954-1955	Troop Reduction	Number of soldiers reduced to approximately 3.5 million
1975-1978	Troop Reduction	Approximately 13% of the soldiers were reduced compared to 1975

1980	Mostly Non-Combatants Reduction	N/A
1982	PLA Reformation and Troop Reduction	N/A
1985	**Troop Reduction (Under Deng Xiaoping, Chairman of CMC at the time)**	**Approximately 1 million soldiers were reduced (From 4.2 million to 3.2 million)**
1995-1999	Troop Reduction	Approximately 500 thousand soldiers were reduced in 4 years
2003-2005	Troop Reduction	The number of soldiers were reduced to approximately 2.3 million
2017	**Troop Reduction**	**Approximately 2.3 million soldiers were reduced to 2 million**

Among the eleven times of troop reductions, two of them are the most well-known to the world, which are highlighted in the table. In 1985, Deng Xiaoping downsized a whopping 1 million PLA troops. Thirty-two years later, Xi Jinping declared his '300 thousand troop reduction plan' at the 2015 China Victory Day Parade, meaning over one-eighth of the PLA troops will be cut. Putting aside the fact that China is an authoritarian regime, announcing such a disarmament plan at one of China's biggest military parades does convey China's resolve and determination to uphold world peace, telling the world that the military parade is not a 'flex of muscle', rather it was an opportunity for China to proclaim that the country will not be a threat to the rest of the world. Many may oppose that China is only reducing its army size so that the country can focus on improving the equipment quality, however, does China really need to trim its army to improve equipment quality? The poor China before its economic reform might need to reduce the size of its army in order to have more budget to spend on equipment, nevertheless, China's military spending takes much less percentage of GDP than it did before; if China's intentions are dangerous, the country could easily invest more in improving its military gear without reducing the size of its troops.

Despite that it might have something to do with China's serious human rights problems that need to be resolved, the country has been a firm advocate and follower of its foreign policy of 'mutual non-interference in domestic affairs', which can be considered as a strong indication of a nation's nonaggression and resolve to a peaceful development. Ever since 1954, five years after the founding of Red China, Zhou Enlai, the Premier of the country at that time, put forward a set of doctrines called 'Five Principles of Peaceful Coexistence' (和平共处五项原则), governing China's relations with other nations, which translates into the following,

(1) Mutual respect for each other's territorial integrity and sovereignty,

(2) Mutual non-aggression,

(3) Mutual non-interference in each other's internal affairs,

(4) Equality and mutual benefit,

(5) Peaceful co-existence.

Although the principles were first used to reach an agreement with India regarding the issues in Tibet, China has persevered its belief on this policy which was reinforced again by almost every Chinese leader, including Xi. If you pay close enough attention to the announcements and responses made by the Chinese Foreign Ministry and how China votes as one of the five permanent members of the UNSC (United Nations Security Council), you will identify that the current Chinese foreign policy is still based on the previous doctrines introduced in the 1950s, giving priority to not interfering in other nation's domestic affairs and respecting territorial integrity. By sticking to this set of principles, China has hardly been involved in any armed conflicts, especially compared with the US and Russia. Later at the groundbreaking Bandung conference between Asian and African countries in 1955, the Five Principles of Peaceful Coexistence were widely accepted and amalgamated into an adapted form that was carried out by many newly independent, third world countries. The doctrines were the essence of the conference, while the conference was a significant step toward the Non-Aligned Movement (NAM). NAM, commonly acknowledged as the largest politically oriented body in the world, has been contributing to the world's peace tremendously by emphasizing cooperation and the policy of non-interference in internal affairs among nations. If China is to maintain its firm support on the Five Principles of Peaceful Coexistence continually, with many other reasons explained in previous chapters, it is unlikely that the country will have any military conflict with other nations. We would be living in an even better world if the whole world could adopt the same doctrines, perhaps like the former Prime Minister of India Jawaharlal Nehru once commented, "If these principles were recognized in the mutual relations of all countries, then indeed there would hardly be any conflict and certainly no war."

While this chapter might be longer than the others, my main points can easily be merged to one sentence that is the Chinese military is not capable of starting a conflict, nor does the Chinese government wish to start a conflict.

CHAPTER IV

WHAT CAME WITH THE RISE OF CHINA?

While the instability of China's economy and the incapability of China's military substantiate the rise of China as peaceful and harmless, it is time to survey what came with China's rise. We are not looking at the great inventions brought by the Chinese civilization, rather, to call the rise of China as an opportunity that benefits the world, it is imperative to examine what has happened since China started to grow expeditiously.

GLOBAL POVERTY REDUCTION

Here is the most apparent benefit brought by the rise of China to the rest of the world, poverty elimination. At the beginning of the 1990s, around half of the population in the global south lived on less than 1.25

USD per day. Approximately 20 years later, just about 700 million people had been lifted out of poverty, marking a successful beginning of the United Nations' Millennium Development Goals (MDG) of reducing poverty, and China is among the biggest contributors of poverty elimination. It is not even necessary to look at how much poverty has been alleviated in China. From the 1990s to 2010s, with the rapid growth of China, the country has lifted over 400 million of its people out of extreme poverty; supporting almost 20 percent of the world population with less than 10 percent of world's farmland, China had already reached all the MDGs by 2015.

China welcomed foreign trade soon after its economic reform. After China joined the World Trade Organization (WTO), the country's average tariffs have dropped massively. Preliminarily, China allowed foreign investment in its exclusive economic zones which are often large urban areas, and the positive result of welcoming foreign investment in these locations later led to a more comprehensive 'door opening' policy in the entirety of China, making China one of the largest receivers of foreign investment. China has become the factory of the world, providing labor and market to foreign countries, at the same time, the opening up of Chinese economy has fueled the unprecedented poverty eradication, immensely contributing to the world economic growth.

Famine and poverty are no longer a part of China's 'export' to the world. Instead, China is now 'exporting' the experience and knowledge of eliminating poverty to the globe. China's success in eradicating poverty has been inspiring and guiding other countries in the global south in its progress of poverty elimination. China, as one of the first upholders of global organizations like the International Labour Organization (ILO), is now cooperating with these organizations to eliminate the world's remaining poverty. As the largest economy in the South-South Cooperation, China has been exploring various ways to share its expertise and successful experience in lifting people out of poverty with its fellow developing countries, which will be further examined in the following paragraph. Certainly, there are still many topical problems that the world needs to resolve, but most of today's problems that we are facing are no longer the same dreadful difficulties such as famine and extreme poverty which we encountered decades ago, on account of the rise of China. In a not too distant future, perhaps, poverty will soon become a history of human civilization.

Theoretically, China's economic development and poverty deduction success have also augmented the mentalities of its fellow developing countries, expanding the policy alternatives of others by showing diverse ways of development. Throughout its vigorous involvement in regional matters, China has also helped its neighbors to attract more attention from the international community.

Besides poverty reduction, undoubtedly, the rise of China has benefited the economic growth and development of its neighboring countries as well.

During the 2008 financial crisis, the world economy was devastated, and many Western countries are still affected by the aftershock of the debt crisis. However, China and those countries that were in close relationship with China were not affected as much. Ever since the financial crisis, China has been vigorously promoting its 'One Belt One Road Initiative (OBOR),' sharing the country's rapid development experience and attempting to stimulate infrastructure construction which previous international financial organizations were not willing or unable to be part of the project. As a legacy of the ancient 'Silk Road' and a brainchild of Xi Jinping, the OBOR initiative first focused on improving infrastructure in terms of transportation. For example, in East Africa's Kenya, China has already invested billions of dollars by assisting Kenya to build its Mombasa-Nairobi Standard Gauge Railway which could not only stimulate the local economy but also assist East African industries and trade between the two continents. In Pakistan, constant power cuts due to the insufficient electricity have always been a difficulty for the developing country. The OBOR allowed Chinese companies and scientists to enter Pakistan and team up with the local scientist to construct the country's largest hydropower station, Nehru Tim Jielu Mu, providing electricity to a large portion of the country's residence. Besides providing power, such a large hydropower station could facilitate Pakistan's economic development in many other ways. Bordering China's Uygur Autonomous Region, the land-locked country Kazakhstan is also one of the beneficiaries of the OBOR. The OBOR connects Kazakhstan and China in a much more efficient way, allowing record-breaking cross-border trade. As one of the largest foreign investors of Kazakhstan, China, along with its OBOR, has invested over 14 billion USD in only ten years. Because of the OBOR investments, Central Asian countries like Kazakhstan are now able to promote themselves as attractive markets for the US and other global investors; the newest investments include the 20 commercial contracts signed between the US and Kazakhstan that are worth approximately 7.5 billion USD. Kenya, Pakistan, and Kazakhstan are only among the first wave of pensionaries of the OBOR; while the initiative continues to spread, more and more countries will be benefited.

In addition to the tremendous amount of investment to its neighboring nations, China has also become the country that 'exports' the most tourists. The Chinese tourists, after ditching poverty and getting richer, are coming out of China to tour, shop, and eat in other countries. Chinese travelers are filling up hotel rooms and cruise liners, and they can be seen at almost all the international airports and train stations. Luxury goods industry has been promoted, and the tourism industry has been reintroduced to a new level by the Chinese. Even though China's household debt is growing rapidly, traveling and shopping abroad has become an essential activity for the Chinese. Already the largest spender on international tourism, China is not showing a single sign of slowing down its export of tourist to the world. Take Chinese visitors to Japan from 2014 to 2015 for example, in the previous year, there were around 2.4 million Chinese citizens visited

Japan, and in 2015, the Chinese visitor arrival number rose to almost 5 million, marking a growth rate of 107 percent year over year. In 2017, the number rose to over 7 million. Up until now, Chinese citizens visiting Japan are still required to have a visa on their passport; picture the number of Chinese travelers if the requirement for a visa is waived. To describe Chinese visitors' massive shopping sprees, the Japanese even coined a new phrase called 爆買い (bakugai), which literally translates to 'explosive shopping.' A booming tourism industry means more employment opportunities, and China has certainly made tourism healthier in many countries through its large number of tourists, and both direct and indirect contribution from China's tourists to other countries' economy is beyond measurement.

After four decades of striving to develop, China is no longer stalling the world economy, and in actuality, China has now become the most substantial driver of global economic growth. After a successful poverty reduction, in terms of economy and numbers, China is now assisting other developing countries to grow in numerous ways. The fact that the rise of China is beneficial to the world is indisputable, and the amount of economic benefit brought by it is tremendous.

To World Peace

In the past five years, Xi Jinping and the Chinese state media have been boasting China's increased effort and achievements in making the world a peaceful place. Although there has always been a certain amount of social instability within China, the country has become one of the largest contributors to world peace; the Chinese state media is stating the truth on this one.

Unlike the United States, China did not send any of its troops or build any military bases to intervene in other nation's domestic affairs after it gained the power to do so. Instead, continued support to the UN has become China's way of getting back to the world. In comparison to the cutback moves and claims made by Trump's administration vis-à-vis the UN, the increasing endeavors to support the UN is making China the new leader and the predominant contributor of UN peacekeeping. In terms of sending and deploying personnel to UN peacekeeping operations, China is already the No.1 benefactor among the five permanent members of the UNSC. Since the beginning of the 1990s, the country has stationed some over 35,000 personnel abroad for UN peacekeeping missions. From 2012 to 2018, fiscally, China has raised its annual contribution to the UN peacekeeping operations from 3.9 percent to over 10 percent, surpassing Japan as the second-largest financial supporter.

China has become one of the leaders in anti-piracy operations since its repaid development of naval force. As a significant player in countering piracy at a global scale, China and its contribution to piracy elimination is more than visible. Yes, one might wonder what the real motives behind China's PLA navy are, and one might speculate that China is very possibly attempting to establish a long-term tenancy for its navy due to the fact that a very large amount of China's crude oil and petroleum importations will have to pass through critical locations such as the Gulf of Aden and the Bab-el-Mandeb Strait. However, up until now, the massive anti-piracy efforts conducted by China still cannot be proven as driven by national interests since nothing that disobey the idea of a free, open and secure global maritime commons has happened yet, at least not in the horn of Africa. Even if China's motives are eventually proven to be non-altruistic, the country still does not have the capability to take the place or even challenge the role of the United States, as mentioned in the previous chapter, let alone the proximity and strength of NATO and the other U.S. led coalition forces. What we do see is the apparent decrease of the number of piracy incidents since China has sent its naval ships for anti-piracy; in 2016, the piracy and armed robbery against ships incidents have dropped to its lowest levels in two decades, according to the International Chamber of Commerce's International Maritime Bureau (IMB).

COMMUNITY OF SHARED FUTURE FOR MANKIND

Without China, globalization is only seeming further and further away in recent years since there are obvious signs of 'de-globalization' happening among other important players around the world. UK's withdrawal from the European Union, the election of Donald Trump, and the many renouncements of important organization like TPP and vital accord such as the Paris Agreement made later by the Trump's administration, are indicating that perhaps we are now in a time of 'de-globalization.' Under America's change of 'direction,' the world is seemingly in need of a new core to bear the leadership and burdens.

The Community of Shared Future for Mankind (人类命运共同体), a brainchild of former Chinese President Hu Jintao, is now constantly emphasized and promoted by President Xi. As the name suggests itself, the concept advocates a fresh structure of international relations, advocating the significance of globalism and the necessity to strengthen global governance. It was not easy for the Chinese government to finally shift its foreign policy from obvious self-orientation to this entire humankind-concentrated direction. Despite the fact that the country itself is still not substantial and steady enough to take the role of looking after the whole world, China shows its determination by inventing and reaffirming the concept of 'The Community of Shared Future for Mankind', and China demonstrates its action to uphold the concept by establishing initiatives like OBOR, AIIB, and assuming leadership roles in them.

Again, although the capacity of China to turn the tide remains unknown, what China put there is beneficial and fruitful. Much of the world has benefited from the rise of China, and China is now planning to let the entire world succeed together with each other's help through China's new framework. Perhaps, compared to the US, China is rather fragile and not as giant, but the country is apparently trying to bear the burdens as the US shifts its direction the other way, and a rising non-western country attempting to assist other countries should not be portraited as a threat.

People, not just Westerners anymore, are concerned that the Chinese are setting up 'honeytraps' through its AIIB and OBOR initiative by putting developing nations in debt, and they believe that the rise of China is simply threatening to the world. Yes, people may have their reasons to explain their beliefs, but perhaps, the first chapter of this book, explains why many would possess such position even without apprehending the context of China and its deeds. Of course, in a distant future, it is possible that China might truly become today's America which has the power and the capacity to 'care' about the others, however, the current China and the China in the foreseeable future does not possess the aptitude to do so, as examined in previous chapters, both in terms of military power and economic/social stability. Conceivably, this writing might be subverted, but what can never be subverted is that the world is always better off only in times of peace, not war.

Notes:

Chaper1: The History of Sinophobia

1 Thomas Harrison, *Greeks and Barbarians* (2002), p. 3.

2 Tim Yang, *The Malleable Yet Undying Nature of the Yellow Peril* (2004).

3 John C. G. Rohl, *The Kaiser and His Court: Wilhelm II and the Government of Germany* (, 1995), p. 203.

4 Peter Thompson, Robert Macklin, *The Man who Died Twice: The Life and Adventures of Morrison of Peking* (2005), p. 190.

5 William Wei, *The Chinese-American Experience: An Introduction* (2014).

6 Bean, CEW, *ANZAC to Amiens* (2014), p. 5.

7 John Mearsheimer, *the Tragedy of Great Power Politics* (2001).

8 Hermann Knackfuß, *Völker Europas, Wahrt Eure Heiligsten Güter* (1895).

9 Phillip May, *The Mongolian Octopus: His Grip on Australia* (1886).

10 Karen Humes, Nicholas Jones, Roberto Ramirez, *Overview of Race and Hispanic Origin: 2010* (2011).

11 John Kuo Wei Tchen, Dylan Yeats, *Yellow Peril! An Archive of Anti-Asian Fear* (2014), p.200-220.

12 Rob Bricken, *Marvel's Attempts to Justify Dr. Strange's Whitewashing Are Getting Insulting* (2016).

13 Kelly Lawler, *Netflix's 'Death Note' adaptation draws backlash for whitewashing* (2017).

14 Landström Björn, *Columbus: The Story of Don Cristóbal Colón, Admiral of the Ocean* (1967), p.27.

15 Raymond Beazley, *Prince Henry the Navigator, the Hero of Portugal and of Modern Discovery, 1394-1460 A.D.: With an*

Account of Geographical Progress Throughout the Middle Ages as the Preparation for His Work (2007). p.14.

16 Alain Peyrefitte, *The Immobile Empire* (2013), p.2-15.

17 Ch'ien Lung Letter to George III (1792), Retrieved 2018.

18 Edward Dickinson, *Sex, Masculinity, and the 'Yellow Peril': Christian von Ehrenfels' Program for a Revision of the European Sexual Order*, 1902–1910 (2002).

19 John Dower, *War Without Mercy: Race & Power in the Pacific War* (1993), p.159.

20 Gina Marchetti, *Romance and the "Yellow Peril": Race, Sex, and Discursive Strategies in Hollywood Fiction* (1994), p.3-5.

21 Jane Burbank, Frederick Cooper, *Empires in World History: Power and the Politics of Difference* (2010), p.43-46.

22 David Morgan, *The Mongols* (2007), p.5.

23 Victor Lieberman, *The Qing Dynasty and Its Neighbors: Early Modern China in World History* (), p.288.

24 Edward Dreyer, *Zheng He: China and the Oceans in the Early Ming Dynasty, 1405-1433* (2007), p.123-126.

25 Robert Finlay, The Voyages of Zheng He: Ideology, State Power, and Maritime Trade in Ming China (2008), p.325-330.

26 József Szabó, Lóránt Dávid, Denes Loczy, *Anthropogenic Geomorphology: A Guide to Man-Made Landforms* (2010), p.220.

27 Li Xiaobing, *A History of the Modern Chinese Army* (2007), p. 205–240.

28 Kaegan McGrath, Vasileios Savvidis, *UNSC Resolution 1887: Packaging Nonproliferation and Disarmament at the United Nations* (2009).

Chapter II: The Chinese Economy and Social Stability

1 International Monetary Fund, *Country Data on the People's Republic of China* (2018).

2 Ravi Kanbur, *Chinese income inequality as measured by the Gini coefficient* (2007) .

3 Xiaoping Deng, Tianjin Report, (The 14th National Congress of the Communist Party of China, 1992).

4 Percy Bysshe Shelley, *A Defence of Poetry, from the Harvard Classics: English Essays: Sidney to Macaulay* (1909-14).

5   Teng   Margaret   Fu,   *Unequal   Primary   Education Opportunities in Rural and Urban China* (2005).

6 The World Bank, *Estimates based on the United Nations Population Division's World Urbanization Prospects* (2018).

7 Spencer   Sheehan,   *China's   Hukou   Reforms   and   the Urbanization Challenge (*2017).

8 National Bureau of Statistics of China, *GDP Annual by Province/Region,* (2018).

9 U.S. Bureau of Economic Analysis, *Total Gross Domestic Product for Kentucky*, (Federal Reserve Bank of St. Louis, 2018).

10 China Academy Index, *China 100 City Price Index Report*, SouFun Holdings Ltd, 2018.

11 United States Home Prices & Values, Zillow Research, 2018. https://www.zillow.com/home-values/.
https://tradingeconomics.com/china/households-debt-to-gdp

12 The New York Times, *New labor law introduced in China,* (2008).

13 China Households Debt to GDP, Trading Economics, Bank for International Settlements, (2018).

14 The World Bank, World Bank national accounts data, and OECD National Accounts data files, GDP Annual Growth of China, 2018.

15 The World Bank, GNI per capita, PPP (current international $), International Comparison Program database, (2017).

16 Malcolm Scott, Cedric Sam, *Here's How Fast China's Economy Is Catching Up to the U.S.,* (2016).

17 Xiaoyi, Mu, *Is Xi Jinping's anti-corruption campaign bringing more corruption?* (2014). Translated by Shaoyu Yuan. The news was posted on the Voice of America's Chinese edition.

18 Confucius (Kong Zi), *The Book of Rites (Li Ji) : English-Chinese Version*, Translated by James Legge, Edited by Dai Sheng.

19 James Legge, *Sacred Books of the East: The Li Ki*, (1885).

20 National Bureau of Statistics of China: China Statistical yearbook   2018,   chapter   2   Population.
http://www.stats.gov.cn/tjsj/ndsj/2018/indexeh.htm

Chapter III: Chinese Military: Weaker than you think and inadequate for conflict

1 Mihai Andrei, *Why 90% of China's youth suffer from near-sightedness*, (2017).
2 David Logan, *China's 'Mystery Warriors'*, (2013).
3 Thomas Bickford, *Regularization and the Chinese People's Liberation Army: An Assessment of Change*, (2000) p. 456-474.
4 Nan Tian, Aude Fleurant, Alexandra Kuimova, Pieter D Wezeman, Siemon T Wezeman, *Fact Sheet: Trends in World Military Expenditure 2017*, (2018).
5 Chun Han Wong, *The Minuscule Cost of Equipping a Chinese Soldier*, (2014).
6 The Associated Press, *GI's gear costs 100 times more than in WWII*, (2007).
7 Hannah Beech, *Military Expansion: China's Soldiers Outgrow Their Tanks and Guns*, (2014).
8 The Associated Press, *Soldiers sized up: Army survey for uniforms, armor*, (2015).
9 Xiaobing Li, *Border Conflicts and the Cultural Revolution*, (2007).
10 David Auerswald, Stephen Saideman, *NATO in Afghanistan: Fighting Together, Fighting Alone*, (2014) p. 87-88.
11 David Stahel, *Operation Barbarossa and Germany's Defeat in the East*, (2009).
12 Karl-Heinz Frieser, *The Blitzkrieg Legend: The 1940 Campaign in the West*, translated by J. T. Greenwood, (2013).
13 Joint Chiefs of Staff, *Doctrine for the Armed Forces of the United States*, Joint Publication 1, Department of Defense, (2000).
14 Yasuyuki Sugiura, *The Joint Operation Structure of the Chinese People's Liberation Army with Focus on the Reorganization of the Chain of Command and Control under the Xi Jinping Administration*, (2017).
15 Phillip Saunders, John Chen, *Is the Chinese Army the Real Winner in PLA Reforms?*, Joint Force Quarterly 83, (2016).
16 Chase, Michael S., Jeffrey Engstrom, Tai Ming Cheung, Kristen A. Gunness, Scott Warren Harold, Susan Puska, and Samuel K. Berkowitz. *Weaknesses in People's Liberation Army Organization and Human Capital: In China's*

Incomplete Military Transformation: Assessing the Weaknesses of the People's Liberation Army (PLA), (2015), p.43-68.

17 Josh Chin, *Chinese General Who Faced Graft Inquiry Dies of Cancer*, (2015).

18 Angela Meng, *Gold, liquor, and houses: new details emerge of disgraced general Gu Junshan's graft loot*, (2014).

19 Ben Blanchard, *China jails former top military officer for life in graft case*, (2016).

20 Chase, Michael S., Jeffrey Engstrom, Tai Ming Cheung, Kristen A. Gunness, Scott Warren Harold, Susan Puska, and Samuel K. Berkowitz. *Weaknesses in People's Liberation Army Organization and Human Capital: In China's Incomplete Military Transformation: Assessing the Weaknesses of the People's Liberation Army (PLA)*, (2015), p.43-68.

21 David Brunnstrom, *North Korean media issues rare criticism of China over nuclear warnings*, (2017).

22 Tayyeb Shabbir, *Financial and Economic Impact of the Global Financial Crisis of 2007-2009 on Pakistan*, (2011).

23 Daniel Runde, *An Economic Crisis in Pakistan Again: What's Different This Time?*, (2018).

24 Seokwoo Lee, *Territorial Disputes Among Japan, China and Taiwan Concerning the Senkaku Islands*, (2002), p.10-13.

25 Robert Beckhusen, *China's Aircraft Carrier Trouble—Spewing Steam and Losing Power*, (2014).

26 Shicun Wu, *Solving Disputes for Regional Cooperation and Development in the South China Sea: A Chinese Perspective*, Chandos Asian Studies Series. (2013).

27 Jane Perez, Beijing's South China Sea Claims Rejected by Hague Tribunal, (2016).

28 Nan Tian, Aude Fleurant, Alexandra Kuimova, Pieter D Wezeman, Siemon T Wezeman, *Fact Sheet: Trends in World Military Expenditure 2017*, (2018).

29 The Chosunilbo, *China Chafes at Korean Observatory on Reef Island*, (2006).

30 U.S. Mission to ASEAN, The statement was found under Education & Culture section of the website, titles Expanding Maritime Cooperation.

31 Mayuko Tani, *ASEAN to start naval exercise with US in 2019*, (2018).
32 Steven Myers, Ellen Barry, Max Fisher, *How India and China Have Come to the Brink Over a Remote Mountain Pass*, (2017).
33 Taylor Fravel, *Regime Insecurity and International Cooperation*, International Security, (2005), p.46-83.
34 Stockholm International Peace Research Institute, *Armaments, Disarmament and International Security*, (2007), p. 555–556.
35 Daniel Barenblatt, *A Plague upon Humanity*, (2004), p. 173.
36 Nuclear Threat Initiative, Country Profiles: China, 2014 (Last updated time).
37 The data and numbers were collected from numerous resources, mostly from PLA Dailyand BBC Chinese by Wen Li in 2015, written in Chinese. News Focus: The Disarmaments of China's Military.
38 Five Principles of Peaceful Coexistence, United Nations Treaty Series, (1954), pp. 57-81.
39 Wenfu Mou, *Five Principles 'still offer solid basis for peace*, Chinese Social Sciences Today, (2015).

Chapter IV:

1 Raj M Desai, *Social Policy and the Elimination of Extreme Poverty, In The Last Mile in Ending Extreme Poverty*, (2015), pp. 301-327.
2 Ministry of Foreign Affairs of the People's Republic of China, *Report on China's Implementation of the Millennium Development Goals (2000-2015)*, (2015).
3 Jinghua Cao, *Facilitate B&R Development with Science*, (2018).
4 Government of the Republic of Kazakhstan, *Minister of Foreign Affairs outlines priorities with regards to the Asian region*, (2017).
5 Evelyn Cheng, *Kazakhstan pushes for US deals — helped by China's investments*, 2018.
6 Japan Tourism Statistics, Trends by Country/Area, *Trends in annual Visitor Arrivals to Japan by Country/Area*, (2019).

https://statistics.jnto.go.jp/en/graph/#graph--trends--by--country

7 Marc Lanteigne, *The Role of U.N. Peacekeeping in China's Expanding Strategic Interests*, (2018).

8 Kuala Lumpur, *Sea piracy drops to 21-year low, IMB reports*, International Chamber of Commerce's International Maritime Bureau (2016).

Bibliography:

Andrei, Mihai, Why 90% of China's youth suffer from near-sightedness, ZME Science, 2017.

Auerswald, David. Saideman, Stephen. NATO in Afghanistan: Fighting Together, Fighting Alone, Princeton University Press, 2014.

Barenblatt, Daniel, A Plague upon Humanity, HarperCollins, 2004.

Bean, CEW, ANZAC to Amiens, Penguin, 2014.

Beazley, Raymond, Prince Henry the Navigator, the Hero of Portugal and of Modern Discovery, 1394-1460 A.D.: With an Account of Geographical Progress Throughout the Middle Ages as the Preparation for His Work, Dodo Press, 2007.

Beech, Hannah, Military Expansion: China's Soldiers Outgrow Their Tanks and Guns, Time, 2014.

Beckhusen, Robert, China's Aircraft Carrier Trouble— Spewing Steam and Losing Power, War is Boring, 2014.

Bickford, Thomas A, Regularization and the Chinese People's Liberation Army: An Assessment of Change, Asian Survey, 2000.

Björn, Landström, Columbus: The Story of Don Cristóbal Colón, Admiral of the Ocean, Macmillan Company, 1967.

Ben Blanchard, China jails former top military officer for life in graft case, Reuters, 2016.

Bricken, Rob, Marvel's Attempts to Justify Dr. Strange's Whitewashing Are Getting Insulting, Gizmodo, 2016.

Brunnstrom, David, North Korean media issues rare criticism of China over nuclear warnings, Reuters, 2017.

Burbank, Jane. Cooper, Frederick, Empires in World History: Power and the Politics of Difference, Princeton University Press, 2007.

Cao, Jinghua, Facilitate B&R Development with Science, Technology and Education, Bureau of International Cooperation, Chinese Academy of Sciences, 2018.

Chase, Michael S., Jeffrey Engstrom, Tai Ming Cheung, Kristen A. Gunness, Scott Warren Harold, Susan Puska, and Samuel K. Berkowitz, Weaknesses in People's Liberation Army Organization and Human Capital: In China's Incomplete Military Transformation: Assessing the Weaknesses of the People's Liberation Army (PLA), Calif.: RAND Corporation, 2015.

Cheng, Evelyn, Kazakhstan pushes for US deals — helped by China's investments, CNBC, 2018.

Chin, Josh, Chinese General Who Faced Graft Inquiry Dies of Cancer, The Wall Street Journal, 2015.

China Academy Index, China 100 City Price Index Report, SouFun Holdings Ltd, 2018.

Ch'ien Lung Letter to George III (1792), University of California Santa Barbara, Retrieved 2018.

Confucius (Kong Zi), The Book of Rites (Li Ji) : English-Chinese Version, Translated by James Legge, Edited by Dai Sheng, Intercultural Press.

Deng Xiaoping, Tianjin Report, The 14th National Congress of the Communist Party of China, 1992.

Desai, Raj, Social Policy and the Elimination of Extreme Poverty, In The Last Mile in Ending Extreme Poverty, edited by Chandy Laurence, Kato Hiroshi, and Kharas Homi, Brookings Institution Press, 2015.

Dickinson, Edward, Sex, Masculinity, and the 'Yellow Peril': Christian von Ehrenfels' Program for a Revision of the European Sexual Order, 1902–1910, German Studies Review, 2002.

Dower, John. War Without Mercy: Race & Power in the Pacific War, New York: Pantheon, 1993.

Dreyer, Edward, Zheng He: China and the Oceans in the Early Ming Dynasty, 1405-1433, Pearson Longman, 2007.

Finlay, Robert, The Voyages of Zheng He: Ideology, State Power, and Maritime Trade in Ming China, Journal of the Historical Society, 2008.

Fravel, Taylor, Regime Insecurity and International Cooperation, International Security, The President and Fellows of Harvard College and the Massachusetts Institute of Technology, 2005.

Frieser, Karl-Heinz, The Blitzkrieg Legend: The 1940 Campaign in the West, translated by J. T. Greenwood, Naval Institute Press, 2013.

Fu, Teng Margaret, Unequal Primary Education Opportunities in Rural and Urban China, China Perspectives, 2005.

Government of the Republic of Kazakhstan, Minister of Foreign Affairs outlines priorities with regards to the Asian region, 2017.

Harrison, Thomas, ed. Greeks and Barbarians. Edinburgh University Press, 2002.

Humes, Karen. Jones, Nicholas. Ramirez, Roberto. Overview of Race and Hispanic Origin: 2010, United States Census Bureau. United States Department of Commerce, 2011

Japan Tourism Statistics, Trends by Country/Area, Trends in annual Visitor Arrivals to Japan by Country/Area, 2019.

Joint Chiefs of Staff, Doctrine for the Armed Forces of the United States, Joint Publication 1, Department of Defense, 2000.

Kanbur, Ravi, Chinese income inequality as measured by the Gini coefficient, Cornell University, 2007.

Knackfuß, Hermann, Völker Europas, Wahrt Eure Heiligsten Güter, 1895.

Kuo Wei Tchen, John. Yeats, Dylan, Yellow Peril! An Archive of Anti-Asian Fear, Verso, 2014.

Lanteigne, Marc, The Role of U.N. Peacekeeping in China's Expanding Strategic Interests, United States Institute of Peace, 2018.

Lawler, Kelly. Netflix's 'Death Note' adaptation draws backlash for whitewashing, USA Today, 2017.

Lee, Seokwoo, Territorial Disputes Among Japan, China and Taiwan Concerning the Senkaku Islands, International Boundaries Research Unit, 2002.

Legge, James, Sacred Books of the East, volume 28, part 4: The Li Ki, 1885.

Li, Xiaobing, Border Conflicts and the Cultural Revolution, University Press of Kentucky, 2007.

Lieberman, Victor. The Qing Dynasty and Its Neighbors: Early Modern China in World History, Social Science History 32, no. 2, 2008.

Logan, David, China's 'Mystery Warriors', The Diplomat, 2013.

Lumpur, Kuala, Sea piracy drops to 21-year low, IMB reports, International Chamber of Commerce, International Maritime Bureau, 2016.

Marchetti, Gina, Romance and the "Yellow Peril": Race, Sex, and Discursive Strategies in Hollywood Fiction, University of California Press, 1994.

May, Philip, The Mongolian Octopus: His Grip on Australia, The Bulletin, 1886.

McGrath, Kaegan, Savvidis, Vasileios UNSC Resolution 1887: Packaging Nonproliferation and Disarmament at the United Nations, Nuclear Threat Initiative, 2009.

Mearsheimer, John, the Tragedy of Great Power Politics, Foreign Affairs, 2001.

Meng, Angela, Gold, liquor, and houses: new details emerge of disgraced general Gu Junshan's graft loot, South China Morning Post, 2014.

Ministry of Foreign Affairs of the People's Republic of China, Report on China's Implementation of the Millennium Development Goals (2000-2015), United Nations System in China, 2015.

Morgan, David, The Mongols, Blackwell Publishing, 2007.

Mou, Wenfu, Five Principles'still offer solid basis for peace, Chinese Social Sciences Today, Social Sciences in China Press, 2015.

Mu, Xiaoyu, Is Xi Jinping's anti-corruption campaign bringing more corruption? Voice of America, 2014. Translated by Shaoyu Yuan.

Myers, Steven, Barry, Ellen, Fisher, Max, How India and China Have Come to the Brink Over a Remote Mountain Pass, The New York Times, 2017.

National Bureau of Statistics of Shina, GDP Annual by Province/Region, 2017.

National Bureau of Statistics of China: China Statistical yearbook 2018, chapter 2 Population, 2018.

Nuclear Threat Initiative, Country Profiles: China, 2014.

Perez, Jane, Beijing's South China Sea Claims Rejected by Hague Tribunal, The New York Times, 2016.

Peyrefitte, Alain, The Immobile Empire, Knopf Doubleday Publishing Group, 2013.

Rohl, John, the Kaiser and His Court: Wilhelm II and the Government of Germany, Cambridge University Press, 1995.

Runde, Daniel, An Economic Crisis in Pakistan Again: What's Different This Time?, Center For Strategic & International Studies, 2018.

Saunders, Philips. Chen, John. Is the Chinese Army the Real Winner in PLA Reforms?, Joint Force Quarterly 83, National Defense University Press, 2016.

Scott, Malcolm. Sam, Cedric, Here's How Fast China's Economy Is Catching Up to the U.S., Bloomberg, 2016.

Shabbir, Tayyeb, Financial and Economic Impact of the Global Financial Crisis of 2007-2009 on Pakistan, Centre for Public Policy and Governance, 2011.

Sheehan, Spencer, China's Hukou Reforms and the Urbanization Challenge, The Diplomat, 2017.

Shelley, Percy Bysshe, A Defence of Poetry, from the Harvard Classics: English Essays: Sidney to Macaulay, Bartleby.com , 1909-14.

Stahel, David, Operation Barbarossa and Germany's Defeat in the East, Cambridge University Press, 2009.

Stockholm International Peace Research Institute, Armaments, Disarmament and International Security, Oxford University Press, 2007.

Sugiura, Yasuyuki, The Joint Operation Structure of the Chinese People's Liberation Army with Focus on the Reorganization of the Chain of Command and Control under the Xi Jinping Administration, National Institute for Defense Studies, 2017.

Szabó, József; Dávid, Lóránt; Loczy, Denes, Anthropogenic Geomorphology: A Guide to Man-made Landforms, Springer Science & Business Media, 2010.

Tani, Mayuko, ASEAN to start naval exercise with US in 2019, Nikkei Asian Review, 2018.

The Associated Press, GI's gear costs 100 times more than in WWII, NBC, 2007.

The Associated Press, Soldiers sized up: Army survey for uniforms, armor, Fox, 2015.

The Chosunilbo, China Chafes at Korean Observatory on Reef Island, Chosun Media, 2006.

The New York Times, New labor law introduced in China, 2008.

The World Bank, Estimates based on the United Nations Population Division's World Urbanization Prospects, 2018.

The World Bank, GNI per capita, PPP, International Comparison Program database, 2017.

Thompson, Peter and Macklin, Robert The Man who Died Twice: The Life and Adventures of Morrison of Peking. Crow's Nest, Australia: Allen & Unwin, 2005.

Tian, Nan. Fleurant, Aude. Kuimova, Alexandra. Wezeman, Pieter. Siemon T, Fact Sheet: Trends in World Military Expenditure 2017, Stockholm International Peace Research Institute, 2018

United Nations Treaty Series, Five Principles of Peaceful Coexistence, vol. 299, United Nations, 1954.

United States Home Prices & Values, Zillow Research, 2018.

U.S. Bureau of Economic Analysis, Total Gross Domestic Product for Kentucky, Federal Reserve Bank of St. Louis, 2018.

Wei, William, The Chinese-American Experience: An Introduction, University of Colorado at Boulder, 2014.

Wong, Chun Han, The Minuscule Cost of Equipping a Chinese Soldier, The Wall Street Journal, 2014.

Wu, Shicun, Solving Disputes for Regional Cooperation and Development in the South China Sea: A Chinese Perspective. Chandos Asian Studies Series, Elsevier Reed, 2013.

Yang, Tim, The Malleable Yet Undying Nature of the Yellow Peril, Dartmouth College, 2004.

Index

117

119

ABOUT THE AUTHOR

Shaoyu Yuan, as of 2019, is a Ph.D. student at Rutgers University. Yuan received his B.A. from Centre College and his M.S. from Northeastern University.

Born in 1995, Yuan moved to America in 2013 at the age of seventeen. He resides in Fort Lee, New Jersey.